Making History:

A Guide to Writing Historical Fiction

D K Marley

HISTORIUM
BOOKS

Making History:

A Guide to Writing Historical Fiction

Library of Congress Control Number on file

ISBN Paperback 979-8-9883817-9-2

ISBN Ebook 978-1-9624650-8-3

Follow the author:

www.thehistoricalfictioncompany.com

www.facebook.com/therealdkmarley.author

Published by Historium Press

Macon Georgia

www.historiumpress.com

2023

Table of Contents

To Lulu and Buddy

Special thanks to Lorin O. and Jason S.
whose teaching skills never left me.

An Introduction to Historical Fiction

by D. K. Marley

In the realm of historical fiction, an ethereal veil shrouds the distant past, and amidst the shifting sands of time, narratives unfold like ancient scrolls, beckoning readers to tread the corridors of history. Here, I, endeavor to traverse the majestic landscapes of this enigmatic genre, where truth and imagination entwine in a dance as old as humanity itself.

Within the hallowed halls of historical fiction, the echoes of bygone epochs resonate, inviting us to commune with long-forgotten souls. In this sacred space, the veracity of history meets the potency of storytelling, for it is not enough to merely recount the past with a dry recitation of facts; one must infuse it with the ardor of the human spirit. It is the pursuit of this fervor, this unwavering spirit, that drives me to render the past in all its hues and shades.

Historical fiction is not an exercise in mere nostalgia or the retelling of distant happenings. No, it is the delicate art of reviving those forgotten whispers and lost battles, summoning forth the ghosts of heroes and villains alike, and weaving a vibrant tapestry where lives intertwine with events, and destinies collide with circumstance.

Yet, one must tread with humility and reverence on this sacred ground. For every stroke of the pen, the historian and the novelist find themselves enmeshed in an intricate dance, where historical facts mold the contours of the narrative, while imagination breathes life into the shadows of antiquity. In this confluence of realms, the writer becomes a steward of the past, navigating the labyrinth of time with a blend of scholarly rigor and artistic flair.

It is amid these tangled roots of truth and fiction that the essence of human existence blossoms forth. For in the annals of history, we find not only the grandeur of empires but also the tender whispers of love, the searing cries of injustice, and the relentless quest for meaning. Historical fiction, with its immutable allure, peels back the layers of time, revealing our common heritage as beings bound by the tapestry of history.

Thus, as I embark upon this literary journey, I pay homage to the masters who have come before me, whose ink has breathed life into the ages past. I seek to embrace their legacy, to evoke the triumphs and tragedies of generations long gone, and to remind us all that the past, though distant, continues to thread its way through the fabric of our present.

In this pursuit, dear reader, I invite you to walk beside me, hand in hand, as we traverse the corridors of history's palaces and hovels alike. Together, we shall embrace the enigmatic allure of historical fiction, savoring the stories that emerge from the marriage of truth and imagination, and witnessing the eternal dance of humanity across the sands of time.

And as always, "Keep making history and keep writing...."

Chapter 2
Understanding Historical Fiction
Through Tolstoy's Eyes

Much like the sweeping landscapes of Tolstoy's narratives, historical fiction transports us to distant epochs, where reality melds with imagination, and the human spirit transcends temporal boundaries. Let us embark on this literary journey together, where I shall elucidate the essence of historical fiction, its significance, and the profound insights it bestows upon us as readers.

At its core, historical fiction interweaves factual events and figures from the past with the creative weft of storytelling. It is an intricate tapestry that brings historical epochs to life, blending the real with the imagined. The genre is an alchemical fusion of historical accuracy and literary artistry, where authors undertake the Herculean task of recreating bygone eras, capturing their spirit, and breathing life into the shadows of history.

Historical fiction is more than a mere recounting of facts; it encapsulates the zeitgeist of a particular era, evoking the spirit of the times through vivid depictions of customs, cultures, and societal norms. Tolstoy himself accomplished this feat brilliantly in "War and Peace," where he plunged readers into the tumultuous epochs of early 19th-century Russia, imbuing his narrative with authentic historical detail and a profound understanding of the human condition.

Tolstoy's characters are not merely passive observers of history; they embody the era's essence, becoming vessels through which history unfolds. These characters represent the hopes, fears, and aspirations of their respective times, making the past palpable and relatable to modern readers. As we journey with these characters, we traverse the historical landscapes, witnessing both their personal struggles and the grand sweep of historical events.

Now, let us delve into the importance and impact of historical fiction on readers and society as a whole.

Historical fiction serves as a lens through which we can examine the past with fresh perspectives. By breathing life into historical events, it enables us to understand the human elements behind the cold facts and dates. We immerse ourselves in the struggles and triumphs of characters living in eras far removed from our own, fostering empathy and understanding for the diverse experiences of humanity throughout history. Tolstoy's literary masterpieces lead us on this journey of discovery, where we not only learn about historical events but also gain insights into the intricacies of the human psyche.

Interestingly, historical fiction is not confined to the past; it often reflects the concerns and issues of the present. Authors, much like Tolstoy, draw parallels between historical events and contemporary challenges, inviting readers to ponder the continuity of human experiences and the cyclical nature of history. As we read about the struggles of characters in different historical settings, we find echoes of our own lives, prompting us to consider the timeless themes of love, war, ambition, and societal change.

Creating a compelling work of historical fiction requires meticulous research, artistic prowess, and a deep understanding of human nature. Tolstoy's approach to storytelling provides valuable insights into this craft.

Before penning a historical fiction masterpiece, authors must immerse themselves in the annals of history. Diligent research is the foundation upon which the fictional elements are constructed, ensuring historical accuracy and authenticity in the narrative. Tolstoy's commitment to exhaustive research is evident in his works, wherein he delved into various historical sources and firsthand accounts to create a vivid canvas of his chosen era. From the sprawling battlefields to the opulent salons, Tolstoy's attention to detail paints a vivid picture of the past, making the reader feel as if they are experiencing history firsthand.

In historical fiction, every facet must reflect the period being portrayed. From the attire and architecture to the language and customs, the devil resides in the details. Tolstoy's ability to describe minute details and embed them seamlessly into the narrative breathes life into his settings, enriching the reader's experience. The authentic portrayal of historical settings not only enhances the story's realism but also serves as a means of transporting the reader back in time.

The enduring legacy of historical fiction can be witnessed in its ability to transcend time and inspire generations of readers.

Historical fiction plays a vital role in preserving cultural memory. By narrating the stories of the past, it ensures that pivotal moments and forgotten figures are not lost to the ravages of time. Tolstoy's literary legacy exemplifies this preservation, as his works continue to educate and enthrall readers about Russian history and society. Through historical fiction, the voices of the past resonate in the present, and the lessons of history remain relevant for future generations.

Reading historical fiction offers an immersive and engaging mode of learning history. Through the eyes of compelling characters, readers absorb knowledge of the past effortlessly. This form of experiential learning fosters a deeper understanding and appreciation for historical events. Tolstoy's masterpieces remain cherished educational tools in this regard, offering glimpses into the intricacies of Russian society during the Napoleonic era. The power of historical fiction lies in its ability to educate while entertaining, making history come alive for readers of all ages.

The experience of reading historical fiction, much like a pilgrimage, leads readers on a transformative journey.

As readers immerse themselves in the lives of historical characters, they cultivate empathy and understanding for the struggles faced by individuals of the past. This compassionate connection bridges the gap between ages and cultures, fostering a greater sense of shared humanity. Tolstoy's narratives embody this transformative power, prompting readers to see themselves in the grand tapestry of history. As we identify with the hopes, dreams, and fears of historical characters, we gain a broader perspective on our own lives and the collective human experience.

Historical fiction presents a canvas to explore the nuances of human nature—our virtues, vices, strengths, and weaknesses. It compels us to reflect on the recurring themes and patterns that shape human behavior across time. Tolstoy's multidimensional characters, with their flaws and virtues, serve as mirrors to our own selves, encouraging introspection and self-discovery. By contemplating the complexities of historical figures, we are prompted to examine our own values and choices, understanding that the human spirit remains constant, regardless of the era.

In the realm of historical fiction, we traverse time's corridors, navigating the past's labyrinthine corridors with wonder and curiosity. Through the artistry of writers like Tolstoy, the genre grants us passage into forgotten worlds, enabling us to discover the unbroken threads that unite the human experience across epochs. With each turn of the page, historical fiction invites us to savor the wisdom of the ages, understand the intricacies of human history, and glimpse the perennial truths that transcend time itself. The legacy of Tolstoy's literary genius endures as an eternal flame, inspiring writers and readers alike on this ever-evolving voyage through the tapestry of historical fiction.

Using Tolstoy's Techniques in Writing Historical Fiction

Leo Tolstoy, one of the most renowned authors in history, can be immensely helpful for a writer looking to understand writing historical fiction. His magnum opus, "War and Peace," is a classic example of historical fiction that captures the essence of the era it portrays. Here are some key lessons that writers can learn from Tolstoy:

1. Extensive Research: Tolstoy's commitment to research is evident in the meticulous historical accuracy of his work. To write historical fiction effectively, you must conduct thorough research into the time period, setting, culture, customs, political climate, and significant events. This attention to detail will enhance the authenticity of your narrative and immerse readers in the historical world.

2. Complex Characters: Tolstoy's characters are deeply developed and multifaceted, reflecting the complexities of real-life individuals. In historical fiction, characters should feel true to their time while also being relatable to contemporary readers. Developing well-rounded characters with their own desires, conflicts, and motivations adds depth and

realism to the story.

3. Blending Historical and Fictional Elements: Tolstoy masterfully interweaves historical events and real figures with fictional plotlines and characters. Balancing these elements is crucial in historical fiction to provide an engaging narrative while staying true to historical facts. Strive for a seamless blend that captures the essence of the time without getting bogged down in historical exposition.

4. Exploration of Themes: Tolstoy delves into significant themes such as war, love, society, and the human condition in his works. Historical fiction offers an opportunity to explore timeless themes through the lens of a bygone era. Use the historical context to delve into profound themes that resonate with modern readers.

5. Societal and Cultural Context: A strong grasp of the historical context is essential for a writer to portray the norms, traditions, and cultural values of the time accurately. Tolstoy's depiction of Russian society during the Napoleonic era in "War and Peace" is a remarkable example of integrating cultural and societal elements to enrich the narrative.

6. Emphasis on Human Experience: Tolstoy's focus on human emotions and experiences brings his characters to life. Historical fiction should not only narrate events but also explore how those events impact the lives of individuals. By humanizing historical figures and ordinary people alike, you can make the past resonate with contemporary audiences.

7. Handling Multiple Perspectives: "War and Peace" encompasses a wide array of characters and

viewpoints. Tolstoy shows different sides of the same event through various characters, creating a panoramic view of history. In historical fiction, handling multiple perspectives can give a more comprehensive and nuanced understanding of the past.

8. Attention to Language and Style: Tolstoy's writing style is known for its depth and eloquence. Although your writing should suit modern reading preferences, incorporating elements of historical language, idioms, and dialogue can lend authenticity to the historical setting.

By studying Tolstoy's techniques and the way he brings history to life, writers can gain valuable insights into crafting compelling and authentic historical fiction. Remember that while research is essential, the heart of historical fiction lies in connecting readers emotionally with the past, making it both educational and enjoyable.

Chapter 3

In the Footsteps of Time:

Embracing the Viability of Historical Fiction

In a world brimming with possibilities, where the modern tempest of ideas and genres swirls like a kaleidoscope of creativity, there lies an enchanting realm - the world of historical fiction. In the footsteps of time, this genre beckons writers with its timeless charm, presenting a viable and enticing creative path to wander. As Virginia Woolf would muse, the fusion of history and fiction unleashes a potent elixir, fostering a deeper connection with our past, igniting the embers of imagination, and unlocking doors to uncharted narrative territories.

In the tapestry of literature, historical fiction stands as a seamless blend of past and present, where the warp of history intertwines with the weft of imagination. Just as a skilled weaver threads their loom, writers of historical fiction must meticulously research the annals of history, mastering the subtleties of the time period. In this pursuit, they gather forgotten fragments and dusty details, transforming them into a vibrant canvas on which their characters dance.

The task is no less demanding than that of the alchemist, who seeks to transmute base metals into gold. But this very challenge is what draws writers to the genre, for within its complexity lies the allure of discovery. As Virginia Woolf herself would attest, it is the quest to uncover the elusive essence of the past that renders historical fiction a worthy and exciting endeavor.

Historical fiction, like the looking glass of Lewis Carroll's whimsical tale, beckons us to step into an alternate reality. The writer's imagination becomes a portal through which readers are transported across epochs, becoming time-travelers themselves. It is an invitation to wander through palaces and hovels, to breathe the air of bygone centuries, and to forge an empathic connection with long-gone souls.

In the hands of a skilled author, historical fiction becomes a time machine, gifting readers the chance to live the lives of queens and commoners, warriors and poets. The allure lies in this intimate dance with history, where the writer's words become a bridge to the past, stretching across the vast chasm of time.

As a pioneer of literary modernism, Virginia Woolf's voice echoes through the ages, infusing her works with a poetic and imaginative spirit. In historical fiction, her artistic ethos finds an ideal playground. By blending history with the alchemy of fiction, writers become curators of forgotten tales, breathing life into the silent whispers of the past.

Consider the beauty of rendering a long-lost love story, etching an indelible mark on history's canvas. Picture the liberation of an unsung heroine's voice, once stifled by the rigid confines of her time, rising like a phoenix through the pages. Historical fiction weaves a tapestry of emotions and experiences, opening new avenues for creative expression.

In the cacophony of the present, historical fiction serves as a reflective mirror. Just as Virginia Woolf's literature brought forth the complexities of human consciousness, this genre illuminates the resonance of history with our modern sensibilities. History, as a cyclical continuum, finds echoes in our contemporary world, revealing the constants that shape human existence.

By venturing into the past, writers gain insight into the fabric of society, the intricacies of human nature, and the interplay of power and ambition. This exploration sparks conversations about who we are today, giving voice to questions that transcend time and inviting readers to ponder the trajectory of our future.

In the embrace of historical fiction, writers find themselves in a delicate dance with history. It is a genre that requires profound dedication, meticulous research, and a touch of alchemy to weave the strands of the past with the threads of imagination. As Virginia Woolf's legacy reminds us, this creative path is more than viable—it is a doorway to understanding, an exploration of self, and an ode to the timeless symphony of humanity's shared journey. So, as writers embark on this enchanting voyage, they discover that history and fiction are not separate realms, but intertwined facets of the same shining gem.

Stream of Consciousness:
Diving into the Depths of the Past

Writing historical fiction in the style of Virginia Woolf is a captivating and rewarding endeavor, as it allows writers to infuse their narratives with the same poetic brilliance and introspective depth that defined Woolf's own literary legacy. Embracing Woolf's distinctive style in historical fiction opens a gateway to a world of heightened emotions, nuanced characterizations, and a profound exploration of the human psyche amidst the currents of history. Here are some compelling reasons to write historical fiction in the spirit of Virginia Woolf:

Virginia Woolf's stream-of-consciousness technique invites writers to plunge into the minds of historical characters, capturing their innermost thoughts, desires, and fears. By adopting this style, writers can create an intimate connection between readers and historical figures, breathing life into long-gone souls and providing fresh perspectives on familiar historical events. The depth and immediacy of stream of consciousness enrich historical fiction, transforming it into an immersive experience that transcends time.

Woolf's emphasis on sensory impressions infuses her prose with vivid imagery, evoking the sights, sounds, and scents of a bygone era. In historical fiction, this technique can transport readers back in time, immersing them in the rich tapestry of historical settings. Whether it's the bustling streets of ancient Rome, the smoky taverns of Victorian London, or the ethereal courts of Renaissance Europe, the careful portrayal of sensory details transports readers into the heart of history, breathing life into the past.

Woolf's interior monologues offer profound insights into her characters' motivations and emotions. In historical fiction, this technique allows writers to explore the complexities of historical figures, delving into their personal dilemmas and internal conflicts. By understanding the historical context through the lens of inner thoughts, writers can unravel the intricacies of characters' decisions and actions, lending depth and authenticity to their portrayal of the past.

Woolf's exploration of time and memory blurs the boundaries between past and present, illuminating the interconnectedness of all human experiences. In historical fiction, this approach can lead to compelling narratives that seamlessly weave past and present, as characters grapple with the echoes of history in their contemporary lives. By using memory as a thread, writers can draw parallels between historical events and contemporary concerns, making historical fiction a mirror reflecting both the past and the present.

As a pioneering feminist writer, Virginia Woolf brought to light the voices of women, often overlooked in history. Writing historical fiction in her style provides a platform to resurrect forgotten stories of women from different eras, shedding light on their struggles, triumphs, and desires. This approach allows writers to challenge historical patriarchal narratives, reimagining history from a feminist perspective and celebrating the resilience and agency of women throughout time.

Choosing to write historical fiction in the style of Virginia Woolf is a remarkable creative path that breathes new life into the genre. It enables writers to explore history through the lens of human consciousness, to paint sensory-rich portraits of the past, and to unravel the intricate motivations of historical characters. This stylistic approach offers an opportunity to transcend the limitations of time and connect readers with the echoes of history, while also empowering writers to give voice to marginalized perspectives. In embracing Woolf's literary legacy, writers can craft historical fiction that not only enlightens but also resonates deeply with contemporary sensibilities.

Chapter 4

Unraveling the Mystique: Understanding the Timeless Attraction to History

History, like a vast and labyrinthine tapestry, weaves together the threads of the past, presenting an intricate panorama of human endeavors and achievements. Across the ages, the allure of history has captivated human imagination, drawing individuals to explore the annals of time and grapple with the enigma of our shared heritage. The attraction to history transcends geographical boundaries, cultural backgrounds, and epochs, resonating deep within the human psyche.

One of the most fundamental reasons behind the attraction to history lies in the human inclination to seek comfort in the familiar. History serves as a treasure trove of stories from our collective past, tales of triumphs and tribulations, love and loss, and the enduring spirit of humanity. By engaging with historical narratives, individuals find solace in knowing that their own struggles and experiences are not isolated but part of a broader continuum of human existence. The past offers a sense of grounding, anchoring us to our roots and providing a foundation upon which we build our present and future.

History is a realm of perpetual discovery, an uncharted territory ripe with untold stories and hidden gems waiting to be unearthed. The allure of history lies in the excitement of exploration, as researchers, historians, and storytellers unearth forgotten tales, revealing long-lost civilizations, events, and figures. This fascination with discovery fuels a sense of curiosity, driving individuals to investigate and make sense of the past's complexities.

History forms an intrinsic part of individual and collective identities. Understanding our roots and heritage fosters a deeper sense of belonging, grounding us in a shared narrative that transcends generations. The attraction to history is often intertwined with a desire to know one's origins, explore cultural traditions, and preserve ancestral memories. By connecting to our past, we gain insights into the tapestry of our identity, carving a path towards self-discovery and a better understanding of the world around us.

History acts as a mirror reflecting the complexities of human nature. By examining the actions and decisions of our ancestors, we gain insights into the triumphs and failures of the human spirit. The study of history exposes the ebbs and flows of civilization, the consequences of choices made, and the evolution of societal values. This reflection engenders humility, as it reminds us of the frailty and potential greatness of humanity, and inspires introspection, as we contemplate the legacies we leave for future generations.

History is a repository of invaluable lessons, presenting both cautionary tales and inspiring triumphs. As philosopher George Santayana famously said, "Those who cannot remember the past are condemned to repeat it." The attraction to history arises from the desire to learn from the past, avoid the mistakes of our predecessors, and embrace the wisdom distilled from their experiences. By recognizing patterns and understanding the consequences of past actions, we can chart a course towards a better future.

Empathy is a cornerstone of the human experience, and history provides a unique platform for its cultivation. By immersing ourselves in historical accounts, we step into the shoes of those who came before us, experiencing their joys, sorrows, and struggles. The attraction to history arises from the transformative power of empathy, as it enables us to see the world through the eyes of others, fostering compassion and a deeper appreciation for the diversity of human experiences.

History is replete with stories of remarkable achievements that have shaped the course of civilization. From awe-inspiring architectural marvels to groundbreaking scientific discoveries, the human spirit's ingenuity and tenacity shine through. The attraction to history is fueled by the wonder of witnessing the heights to which humanity can ascend, leaving an indelible mark on the world.

The timeless appeal of history lies in its ability to connect the past, present, and future, creating a tapestry of human experiences that resonates across time. Through history, we find comfort in the familiar, embrace the allure of discovery, and forge connections to our identity and heritage. History's mirror reflects the complexities of human nature and provides invaluable lessons to guide our future endeavors. Ultimately, the attraction to history is a journey of wonder, as we marvel at the grandeur of human achievements and embark on an ongoing quest to unravel the mysteries of our shared heritage.

*****

Nostalgia and escapism are two intertwined threads that weave a powerful allure, drawing individuals to the realms of history. The attraction to historical settings is often rooted in the human desire to seek comfort in the familiar, to immerse oneself in the echoes of the past, and to find solace in the embrace of nostalgia. Through the lens of history, individuals embark on a journey of rediscovery, where the past becomes a refuge from the complexities of the present, offering a sanctuary of emotional resonance and a longing for simpler times.

Nostalgia is a sentimental yearning for the past, a wistful remembrance of times gone by. In the context of historical settings, nostalgia is a potent force that tugs at the heartstrings, rekindling memories of cherished moments, places, and experiences. Whether it be through family traditions passed down through generations or cultural heritage enshrined in historical monuments, nostalgia beckons individuals to revisit their roots and relive the cherished memories of their ancestors.

Historical fiction, with its vivid portrayal of bygone eras, serves as a vessel for nostalgia's journey. Authors skillfully transport readers to the sights, sounds, and emotions of another time, evoking a sense of familiarity and belonging. This connection to the past offers a refuge from the chaos of the present, providing solace in a world that often feels fast-paced and unpredictable.

In an age defined by relentless technological advancements and rapid societal changes, escapism becomes a coping mechanism for many. Historical settings provide a much-needed respite from the complexities of modern life, offering a sanctuary where readers can temporarily disconnect from their immediate reality. The allure of history lies in its ability to transport individuals to a simpler, more comprehensible world, where the pace is slower, and the challenges are different.

Historical fiction becomes a portal to these refuge worlds, guiding readers away from their everyday burdens and immersing them in the rich tapestry of the past. As the weight of the present lifts, individuals find themselves engrossed in the intrigues of ancient civilizations, the elegance of bygone eras, and the romance of historical love stories. This escape allows readers to return to the present with a refreshed perspective, recharged by the timeless wisdom and experiences of history.

Nostalgia and escapism are not solely flights of fancy; they serve a deeper purpose, connecting individuals to their roots and shaping their present identities. By revisiting historical settings, people strengthen their bonds with their cultural heritage, affirming their sense of identity and belonging. Historical fiction, with its meticulous attention to detail, preserves cultural traditions, historical events, and societal norms, serving as a bridge between the past and the present.

Furthermore, the escapism of historical settings serves as a catalyst for creative thinking and problem-solving. As individuals detach from their immediate reality, they open themselves up to new perspectives and insights that can be applied to contemporary challenges. History becomes a source of inspiration, offering lessons, and solutions that have stood the test of time.

While the allure of historical settings through nostalgia and escapism is undeniable, it is crucial to strike a balance between the past and the present. Overindulgence in nostalgia can lead to romanticizing history, blurring the lines between fact and fiction. This romanticization can sometimes overlook the harsh realities of the past, glossing over the struggles of historical figures and marginalized communities.

Similarly, excessive escapism may lead to a disconnection from the responsibilities of the present and a reluctance to confront contemporary issues. While historical fiction can offer respite, it is essential to recognize that the challenges of the past were no less daunting than those of today.

The allure of historical settings through nostalgia and

escapism is a timeless human inclination. By seeking comfort in the familiar and escaping to the past, individuals find solace and inspiration in the echoes of history. Nostalgia serves as a bridge to our roots, connecting us with our cultural heritage, while escapism offers a sanctuary from the complexities of modern life. As history becomes a refuge, its wisdom guides us forward, imparting valuable lessons from the past to shape our present and future endeavors. Yet, it is essential to tread the path of history with discernment, acknowledging its complexities and learning from its triumphs and tragedies, to truly harness its transformative power.

*****

The allure of history lies not only in the comfort of the familiar but also in the boundless fascination with unexplored worlds. The human spirit is inherently curious, driven by an insatiable desire to uncover the unknown, to venture beyond the confines of the present, and to embrace the thrill of discovery. Historical settings, with their vast expanse of untold stories and hidden treasures, become an irresistible playground for this innate sense of exploration, offering writers and readers alike a journey of enlightenment and wonder.

History is a vast tapestry woven over millennia, and while some threads shine brightly in the collective consciousness, many others lie obscured, waiting to be unearthed. The fascination with unexplored worlds in historical settings stems from the desire to shed light on forgotten narratives and to breathe life into obscured characters and events. Like intrepid archaeologists, writers embark on a quest to dig through dusty archives, decipher ancient manuscripts, and recover the fragments of history that have eluded public consciousness.

Through historical fiction, these unexplored worlds are revitalized, and their significance is rekindled. Whether it be the stories of marginalized communities, unsung heroes, or overlooked milestones, the appeal of discovery enables writers to bridge the gap between the past and the present, reweaving the fabric of history to include the previously unnoticed and marginalized.

History is a repository of mysteries that pique human curiosity. From unsolved enigmas to unexplained events, the appeal of discovery lies in the joy of unraveling historical puzzles. Historical fiction offers a captivating platform for writers to explore these mysteries, employing their creative ingenuity to propose plausible solutions or to offer alternative interpretations.

By engaging with historical puzzles, writers stimulate readers' critical thinking and foster a sense of intellectual satisfaction. As readers immerse themselves in the narrative, they become part of the exploration, piecing together clues and drawing their conclusions. The thrill of discovery thus becomes an interactive experience, connecting readers with the characters and events of the past, and empowering them to engage with history as active participants in the journey of discovery.

Unexplored worlds in historical settings carry an aura of romance, an allure that evokes a sense of wonder and awe. The appeal of discovery lies in the magical interplay between imagination and reality, as writers infuse historical fiction with elements of fantasy, mystery, and adventure. This enchanting fusion sparks the reader's imagination, transporting them to far-off lands and bygone eras, where the line between history and myth blurs.

In these unexplored worlds, the ordinary becomes extraordinary, and the mundane transforms into the fantastical. Writers craft narratives that weave the extraordinary into the fabric of the known, inviting readers to ponder the mysteries of the past while savoring the thrill of unearthing new and fantastical realms.

The appeal of discovery extends beyond the confines of the written page; it leaves an indelible mark on the human spirit. Historical fiction, with its fascination for unexplored worlds, ignites intellectual curiosity and leaves readers hungry for knowledge. This legacy of inquiry extends to all aspects of life, encouraging individuals to delve deeper into history, to question prevailing narratives, and to seek a comprehensive understanding of the past.

In the broader context of education, historical fiction serves as a gateway to nurturing a lifelong love for learning. By sparking curiosity and engaging the reader's imagination, it fosters a sense of wonder for the world and its rich history. This legacy of intellectual curiosity becomes an enduring source of inspiration for individuals to explore the depths of the unknown, both within the pages of historical fiction and in their everyday lives.

The appeal of discovery in historical settings is an eternal beacon that guides writers and readers through the corridors of time. It is a testament to the boundless human curiosity, the joy of unearthing forgotten narratives, and the romance of exploring uncharted territories. As writers breathe life into these unexplored worlds, they kindle the flame of intellectual curiosity, fostering a sense of wonder and inspiring a lifelong quest for discovery. The allure of history's unexplored realms beckons us to embark on a journey of enlightenment, transforming the past into an ever-present playground of exploration and growth.

*****

The role of identity and heritage in historical fiction is profound, as it weaves a rich tapestry that connects individuals to their cultural roots, fosters a deeper understanding of their ancestral heritage, and celebrates the diversity of human experience. Historical fiction becomes a vehicle for exploring the complexities of identity, the impact of cultural heritage, and the enduring legacy of historical events on individual and collective consciousness. Through the lens of history, writers and readers alike embark on a transformative journey of self-discovery, reclaiming their identity and embracing the intricate threads of their heritage.

In a world marked by globalization and cultural assimilation, the role of identity in historical fiction serves as a beacon to reconnect with cultural roots that might have been obscured over time. Historical settings evoke a sense of nostalgia for traditions, customs, and beliefs passed down through generations. Through vivid portrayal of historical contexts, writers offer readers an opportunity to rediscover their identity, to rekindle the fading embers of their cultural heritage, and to strengthen their bond with the past.

For many individuals, historical fiction becomes a mirror reflecting their own identity, allowing them to see themselves within the context of history. This exploration enables readers to draw parallels between their own experiences and those of historical characters, fostering empathy and a deeper appreciation for their cultural roots.

One of the vital roles of identity in historical fiction is the amplification of marginalized voices and communities. History, as traditionally recorded, often overlooks or sidelines the experiences of minority groups, women, and other marginalized communities. Through historical fiction, writers can reclaim these lost narratives, giving voice to those who were silenced by the dominant historical discourse.

By reimagining history from diverse perspectives, writers challenge conventional narratives, offering readers a broader and more inclusive understanding of the past. This representation is empowering for readers, particularly for members of marginalized communities who can find strength and affirmation in seeing their stories and struggles acknowledged and honored.

Heritage in historical fiction serves as a wellspring of inspiration, as characters draw strength from the experiences and achievements of their ancestors. By exploring their heritage, characters often find guidance and fortitude to overcome contemporary challenges. This connection to heritage becomes a source of resilience and an anchor during times of uncertainty, as characters draw upon the wisdom and courage of their ancestors.

Historical fiction thus becomes a testimony to the enduring legacy of cultural heritage, demonstrating how the values, traditions, and experiences of the past continue to shape the present and future. This recognition of heritage reinforces a sense of belonging and fosters a deeper understanding of one's place in the world.

Identity in historical fiction is multifaceted, often reflecting the intersectionality of characters' identities. Just as individuals in the real world embody multiple facets of identity, characters in historical fiction grapple with various aspects of self, including race, gender, class, and sexuality. By exploring these complexities, writers portray characters as nuanced individuals, breaking away from stereotypes and one-dimensional representations.

Embracing the complexity of identity in historical fiction enriches the narrative and mirrors the richness of human experience. It emphasizes that historical figures were multifaceted individuals, shaped by the interplay of various factors. This recognition of intersectionality fosters a more comprehensive understanding of history and allows readers to relate to characters on a deeper, more human level.

This exploration of self, heritage, and the enduring legacy of history enriches both writers and readers, fostering empathy, understanding, and a profound appreciation for the diversity of human existence. Ultimately, the role of identity and heritage in historical fiction serves as a testament to the timeless relevance of history, and its power to shape, inspire, and unite the human spirit.

*****

Crafting a historical narrative in fiction is a labor of love that requires meticulous research, a deep understanding of the chosen time period, and a delicate balance between historical accuracy and creative license. The creative process involves transforming historical facts and events into a compelling and immersive story, breathing life into characters, and transporting readers to another time. In this article, we explore the intricacies of the creative process in crafting a historical narrative, from the inception of an idea to the final strokes of the pen.

The journey of crafting a historical narrative begins with a spark of inspiration. Writers may find this initial idea in a historical event, an intriguing figure from the past, or a forgotten corner of history that piques their curiosity. This seed of inspiration becomes the foundation upon which the story will unfold.

The creative process often involves extensive research during this initial phase. Writers delve into historical records, primary sources, and scholarly works to grasp the nuances of the chosen time period. This research is crucial, as it enables writers to create an authentic and immersive world that resonates with readers.

One of the greatest challenges in crafting a historical narrative is striking the delicate balance between historical accuracy and creative freedom. While historical fiction allows for imaginative exploration, it is essential to stay true to the historical context, events, and social norms of the time.

Writers must exercise caution not to distort historical facts for the sake of the plot. However, they may employ creative license in filling in gaps in the historical record or interpreting the motivations of historical figures. The art lies in interweaving fact and fiction seamlessly, creating a narrative that respects the past while offering a fresh and engaging perspective.

Characters are the heart and soul of any narrative, and historical fiction is no exception. The creative process involves imbuing historical figures with life, transforming them from distant figures on a page to relatable and multidimensional individuals.

Developing characters in historical fiction requires a deep understanding of their motivations, beliefs, and societal context. Writers must research not only the major historical figures but also individuals from various walks of life to create a diverse and realistic cast. This process of character development involves empathy, imagination, and a keen sensitivity to the nuances of human nature across time.

A key element of the creative process in crafting a historical narrative is creating an authentic and vivid setting. The historical context should come alive through evocative descriptions, immersive language, and attention to detail. Readers should feel transported to the chosen time period, experiencing the sights, sounds, and emotions of the past.

To achieve this, writers must immerse themselves in the sensory aspects of the time, from the architecture and fashion to the customs and language of the era. By painting a rich and authentic setting, writers create a world that readers can readily inhabit and become fully engaged in the story.

Beyond the surface of historical events and characters, the creative process allows writers to interweave themes that resonate with contemporary audiences. Historical fiction becomes a mirror reflecting timeless human emotions, universal struggles, and enduring themes.

By exploring themes such as love, power, sacrifice, and resilience, writers create a narrative that transcends time. Readers can draw parallels between the past and the present, recognizing the interconnectedness of human experiences across epochs.

As the creative process unfolds, the narrative takes shape, and the plot evolves. Historical fiction is a journey through history, with twists and turns that mirror the complexities of the past. Writers must carefully orchestrate the narrative, maintaining historical authenticity while building tension and drama to keep readers engaged.

The evolution of the plot requires meticulous planning and editing, ensuring that every event and character arc contributes to the overall story's coherence. Writers must pay attention to pacing, avoiding anachronisms, and crafting a satisfying and meaningful conclusion that leaves a lasting impression on readers.

Through compelling characters, vivid settings, and universal themes, historical fiction becomes a mirror reflecting the human experience across time. It is a testament to the power of storytelling, the enduring appeal of history, and the transformative potential of the written word. The artistry of historical fiction lies in its ability to transport readers to the past while leaving an indelible mark on the present.

*****

At the core of historical accuracy in fiction lies thorough research. Writers undertake extensive exploration of primary sources, historical records, and scholarly works to understand the context, events, and social norms of the chosen time period. This research becomes the foundation upon which the fictional elements are built, allowing writers to immerse readers in an authentic historical setting.

By grounding the narrative in well-researched facts, writers create a sense of credibility and authority, enhancing the reader's trust in the story's historical backdrop. This foundation not only provides rich material for storytelling but also helps writers navigate the complexities of the past while crafting a coherent and immersive narrative.

While historical research forms the bedrock of accuracy, historical records may often have gaps or ambiguities. This is where the art of imaginative reconstruction comes into play. Writers utilize creative license to fill in these gaps with plausible scenarios, imagining the inner thoughts, motivations, and dialogues of historical figures.

Imaginative reconstruction should align with the broader historical context and remain within the realm of possibility.

Writers must avoid creating fictional events that contradict well-established historical facts. The goal is not to rewrite history but to enliven it, offering readers a deeper understanding of the characters and events through the lens of the writer's imagination.

Balancing fact and fiction in historical fiction raises ethical considerations. Writers must be sensitive to the potential impact of their creative choices, especially when dealing with real historical figures or traumatic events. The portrayal of historical figures should be respectful and avoid unnecessary defamation or sensationalism.

Incorporating traumatic events, such as wars or atrocities, demands empathy and responsibility. Writers should approach these subjects with care, recognizing the gravity of the historical events while acknowledging the human suffering involved. The goal is not to exploit history for entertainment but to shed light on past realities and their lasting implications.

The portrayal of historical figures is a critical aspect of historical accuracy. Characters in historical fiction should not be one-dimensional stereotypes but complex individuals with human flaws and virtues. Writers should strive to capture the essence of these figures, bringing them to life through a nuanced portrayal of their beliefs, struggles, and ambitions.

By presenting historical figures as multifaceted individuals, writers transcend the limitations of history textbooks, offering readers a deeper understanding of the people who shaped the past. This characterization humanizes historical figures and fosters empathy, allowing readers to connect with the characters on a personal level.

Historical accuracy does not imply an exhaustive recitation of every historical detail. Writers must find a balance between providing sufficient historical context and leaving room for the reader's imagination. Rather than overwhelming readers with a deluge of historical facts, writers should weave these details into the narrative in a way that enhances the story's atmosphere and authenticity.

Leaving gaps in the historical record can also engage readers in the act of exploration, encouraging them to delve further into history on their own. This interactive aspect enhances the reader's connection to the story and fosters a sense of shared discovery.

The art of historical accuracy is not constrained by a rigid adherence to facts but rather by a responsibility to engage readers in a transformative journey through the past. Striking this delicate balance allows historical fiction to be a bridge that connects the present with the past, enriching our understanding of history while celebrating the enduring allure of storytelling. In this intricate dance between fact and fiction, historical accuracy becomes the heartbeat of a narrative that captivates readers and leaves a lasting impact on the collective memory of human experience.

*****

The interweaving of historical and modern themes in fiction is a testament to the timeless relevance of history and its profound impact on contemporary society. Through historical fiction, writers not only transport readers to the past but also invite them to reflect on the parallels between historical events and present-day issues. This blending of the past and the present fosters a deeper understanding of the complexities of human experience and encourages readers to grapple with contemporary challenges through the lens of history.

History is replete with examples of the triumphs and tragedies of human nature. By interweaving historical and modern themes, writers illuminate the universal aspects of the human condition that transcend time. Themes such as love, power, justice, and resilience resonate across epochs, revealing the continuity of human emotions and struggles.

Through historical fiction, readers are reminded that the strengths and flaws of humanity remain consistent throughout history. This reflection on human nature encourages introspection, as readers contemplate the parallels between the characters of the past and individuals they encounter in their daily lives.

Many of the challenges faced by historical figures mirror contemporary issues, such as social injustice, political oppression, and inequality. By intertwining historical struggles with modern themes, writers draw attention to the enduring nature of these issues and their relevance in shaping the present.

Historical fiction becomes a vehicle for examining the roots of contemporary problems, offering insights into how certain issues have evolved or persisted over time. It also allows readers to draw inspiration from historical figures who fought against adversity, providing a sense of hope and agency in addressing modern-day challenges.

History is a repository of valuable lessons, and the interweaving of historical and modern themes allows writers to impart wisdom from the past to address present-day dilemmas. By revisiting historical events and their consequences, readers gain a broader perspective on the repercussions of actions and decisions.

Through historical fiction, writers can prompt critical thinking about the implications of historical events and how they inform contemporary choices. This examination of history's lessons encourages readers to be more mindful and responsible in their decision-making, considering the long-term impact of their actions on society.

The interweaving of historical and modern themes also highlights the continuum of human history and the ever-evolving nature of society. While historical fiction draws attention to enduring issues, it also portrays the changes and progress that have occurred over time.

By juxtaposing historical and modern settings, writers create a sense of continuity, illustrating how the past influences the present and shapes the future. This perspective reinforces the interconnectedness of human experiences and underscores the significance of learning from history to forge a more enlightened future.

The interplay between historical and modern themes fosters empathy and understanding by highlighting shared experiences and struggles. By immersing readers in historical contexts, writers invite them to empathize with the characters' challenges and to recognize the common threads that unite humanity across generations.

Empathy is a powerful catalyst for social change, and historical fiction can serve as a conduit for cultivating compassion and tolerance. As readers identify with characters from different historical periods, they become more open to understanding diverse perspectives in their contemporary lives.

In this dynamic exchange between the past and the present, historical fiction continues to demonstrate its enduring relevance as a medium that not only entertains but also enriches and enlightens. By embracing the interplay between historical and modern themes, writers and readers alike embark on a transformative journey that spans the ages and contributes to the ongoing evolution of human consciousness.

Chapter 5

Fleshing Out the Past:

The Complexities of Historical Figures

Historical figures are not merely names etched in the annals of time; they are complex and multifaceted individuals who grappled with the challenges and triumphs of their era. In historical fiction, fleshing out these figures requires a delicate balance of historical accuracy and imaginative interpretation. Through meticulous research and empathetic understanding, writers breathe life into historical characters, presenting them as three-dimensional beings with hopes, fears, flaws, and aspirations. So, how does an author explore the complexities of historical figures and the art of bringing them to life in the realm of historical fiction?

As stated before, the process of fleshing out historical figures in fiction begins with extensive research. Writers delve into primary sources, biographies, letters, and accounts from the era to gain a comprehensive understanding of the figure's life, context, and motivations. This research forms the foundation upon which the character will be constructed.

By immersing themselves in the historical context, writers can grasp the nuances of the figure's personality, beliefs, and relationships. This understanding allows them to present a realistic portrayal that resonates with the essence of the historical individual.

Historical figures were not simple archetypes but dynamic individuals with intricate inner lives. Writers must move beyond superficial portrayals and delve into the emotional depths of these characters. They should be portrayed as humans with strengths and weaknesses, joys and sorrows, and aspirations and doubts.

Fleshing out the past requires writers to confront the contradictions and complexities of historical figures. Instead of presenting them as heroes or villains, writers must present a nuanced and balanced portrayal that acknowledges both their admirable qualities and their flaws.

Empathy is a crucial aspect of fleshing out historical figures. Writers must place themselves in the shoes of these individuals, attempting to understand their decisions and actions within the context of their time. This empathetic connection enables writers to humanize the characters and make them relatable to modern audiences.

Imagination also plays a significant role in the process. Historical records may not always provide a complete picture of an individual's inner thoughts or emotions. Writers must fill in these gaps with imaginative interpretations that remain consistent with the historical context.

Fleshing out historical figures involves exploring their relationships with other characters in the narrative. These relationships can be based on historical evidence or inferred from the character's personality and circumstances.

Interactions with other characters allow historical figures to reveal different facets of their personality and bring out the complexities of their emotional landscape. These relationships can add depth to the narrative and shed light on the individual's role in historical events.

Historical figures are not static entities frozen in time; they evolve and change over the course of their lives. Writers must consider the figure's growth and transformation over time, capturing the impact of significant events or experiences on their personality and beliefs.

This evolution allows historical figures to feel alive and authentic, as readers witness their development and response to the challenges and opportunities that history throws their way.

Fleshing out historical figures is an art that demands a blend of research, empathy, and imagination. By delving into the complexities of these individuals, writers can present a vivid and authentic portrayal that bridges the gap between the past and the present.

In historical fiction, historical figures cease to be distant shadows of history but become living, breathing beings who continue to influence and inspire. The complexities of their personalities enrich the narrative, inviting readers to connect with history on a profound and intimate level. As writers breathe life into the past, they unveil the vibrant tapestry of humanity's journey, offering readers a window into the hearts and minds of those who shaped the course of history.

Chapter 6

Reimagining Familiar Figures:
Historical Characters in a New Light

Reimagining familiar historical figures is a captivating aspect of historical fiction, offering writers the opportunity to explore alternative perspectives, untold narratives, and hidden layers of complexity. By presenting well-known figures in a new light, writers challenge conventional interpretations and breathe fresh life into the past. This creative approach enriches the historical narrative, sparks curiosity, and encourages readers to view history from a different angle. In this chapter, we delve into the art of reimagining historical characters, the possibilities it opens, and its significance in the realm of historical fiction.

History often leaves gaps in the records, obscuring the experiences of marginalized communities or individuals whose voices were silenced. Reimagining historical figures allows writers to unveil untold perspectives, offering a more inclusive and diverse representation of the past.

By giving voice to lesser-known figures or fictionalizing the inner thoughts of well-known characters, writers expand the historical narrative to encompass a wider range of experiences. This approach fosters empathy and understanding, enabling readers to connect with the past from new and enriching angles.

Throughout history, certain figures have been elevated to the status of legends, surrounded by mythology that obscures their human complexities. Reimagining familiar historical figures allows writers to challenge these mythical portrayals and present a more humanized version of these individuals.

By acknowledging the flaws and vulnerabilities of historical figures, writers create narratives that are more authentic and relatable. This approach dispels the notion of historical figures as unattainable idols and makes them more accessible to contemporary audiences.

Counterfactual scenarios are a powerful tool in reimagining historical figures. Writers can explore "what if" scenarios, imagining how history might have unfolded differently had certain decisions or events taken an alternative course.

By using counterfactuals, writers prompt readers to consider the contingencies of history and the impact of individual actions on the course of events. This exercise in speculation encourages critical thinking and a deeper appreciation for the complexities of historical causality.

Reimagining historical figures allows writers to delve into the human side of these characters, highlighting their emotions, struggles, and personal relationships. This exploration humanizes historical figures, making them more relatable to readers.

Through this lens, historical figures cease to be distant and unapproachable, and readers can identify with their hopes, fears, and aspirations. This deeper connection enhances the emotional resonance of the narrative and engenders a sense of shared humanity across time.

Reimagining historical characters sparks curiosity and encourages readers to delve deeper into history. The creative liberties taken by writers can prompt readers to investigate the historical record, seeking to differentiate between fact and fiction.

In this way, historical fiction becomes a gateway to historical inquiry, fostering a deeper engagement with the past and encouraging readers to develop a more nuanced understanding of history.

Reimagining familiar historical figures is a testament to the transformative power of historical fiction. By presenting alternative perspectives and humanizing these characters, writers breathe new life into the past, inviting readers to embark on a journey of discovery and enlightenment.

Through the art of reimagining, historical fiction becomes a dynamic space that challenges historical mythology, expands the narrative to include marginalized voices, and encourages critical thinking about historical causality. This creative approach allows history to transcend the confines of the past and establishes a bridge between the known and the unknown, the real and the imagined.

Ultimately, reimagining historical characters in a new light illuminates the intricacies of human experience throughout time, forging a timeless connection between the present and the past. It is an invitation to reimagine history and participate in an ever-evolving dialogue with the past that enriches our understanding of the world and ourselves.

Chapter 7
Giving Voice to the Marginalized:
Women, Minorities, and the Forgotten

In the realm of historical fiction, one of the most powerful and transformative aspects is the ability to give voice to the marginalized: women, minorities, and those who have been forgotten or overlooked by the dominant historical narrative. By weaving their stories into the fabric of history, writers challenge the historical silencing of these voices and offer a more comprehensive and inclusive representation of the past.

Throughout history, the experiences and contributions of women, minorities, and other marginalized groups have often been relegated to the margins or entirely erased from the historical record. Historical fiction becomes a vehicle for reclaiming these lost narratives, allowing writers to shed light on the untold stories of the past.

By giving voice to those who have been silenced, writers challenge historical erasure and dismantle the notion that only a select few shaped the course of history. These narratives not only restore agency to marginalized characters but also provide a more nuanced understanding of the diverse tapestry of human history.

Giving voice to the marginalized fosters empathy and understanding among readers. By immersing themselves in the experiences of characters who faced oppression, discrimination, or invisibility, readers develop a more profound appreciation for the challenges these individuals endured.

Through this empathetic connection, readers gain insights into historical contexts and the broader impact of social and political dynamics. This understanding encourages readers to critically examine historical narratives and recognize the biases inherent in traditional accounts of history.

Historically, women, minorities, and other marginalized groups have often been portrayed through stereotypes or one-dimensional representations. Historical fiction disrupts these simplistic portrayals by presenting multidimensional and complex characters.

By exploring the inner lives, motivations, and struggles of marginalized characters, writers challenge stereotypes and showcase the diverse experiences within these groups. This approach encourages readers to question preconceived notions and fosters a more nuanced understanding of the rich tapestry of human identity.

While historical fiction often delves into the struggles faced by marginalized characters, it also celebrates their resilience and triumphs. These narratives highlight the strength, ingenuity, and perseverance of individuals who navigated adversity and fought for their rights and dignity.

The celebration of resilience in historical fiction serves as an inspiration for readers, empowering them to face their own challenges with courage and determination. These narratives become a testament to the indomitable human spirit and the capacity for transformation in the face of adversity.

Giving voice to the marginalized in historical fiction is not only an act of remembrance but also a call for social change. By bringing marginalized narratives to the forefront, writers invite readers to critically examine the legacies of historical injustices and reflect on their contemporary implications.

These narratives challenge readers to confront issues of

inequality, discrimination, and social prejudice. They serve as a reminder that history is not merely a record of the past but a living force that shapes the present and future, urging readers to take action to create a more just and equitable society.

Historical fiction's ability to give voice to the marginalized is a transformative force that reshapes the narrative of history. By reclaiming lost narratives, challenging stereotypes, and celebrating resilience, writers provide a more inclusive and accurate representation of the past.

Through the empathetic connection forged with marginalized characters, readers gain a deeper understanding of historical contexts and social dynamics. This understanding, in turn, prompts critical examination of contemporary issues and a call for social change.

By giving voice to the marginalized, historical fiction becomes an instrument of empowerment, reclaiming history as a shared tapestry of diverse and interconnected stories. It is an invitation to reshape the narrative of the past, recognize the legacy of historical injustices, and forge a path towards a more equitable and compassionate future.

Chapter 8

Choosing Your Historical Era
– Through Steinbeck's Eyes

In the vast ocean of history, there lies an endless array of eras, each teeming with stories waiting to be told. As a historical writer, the choice of the historical era becomes a voyage of discovery, a quest to unearth the untamed past and give voice to the forgotten. Just as a sailor selects the winds that will carry them across uncharted waters, so must the historical writer chart their course through time. As I embark on this journey, I find myself pondering the currents that guide me in choosing the right historical era.

In the restless heart of every historical writer lies a yearning for the unknown, a desire to traverse time's unexplored territories. The allure of an unfamiliar era beckons, promising tales yet untold, characters yet unimagined, and a tapestry of human experience yet uncharted. It is the whisper of history's forgotten voices, urging us to delve into the forgotten pages and resurrect their stories from the annals of time.

As a historical writer, one must dive beyond the surface of history to discern the eras that pulsate with historical depth. It is not enough to skim the waves; we must plunge into the depths where history's secrets lie hidden. The choice of an era with profound historical significance allows us to weave intricate narratives, layer upon layer, where historical fact and creative vision intertwine.

A historical era resonates with the heart of a writer when its echoes reverberate through the corridors of time and touch the chords of our present. It is in this resonance that history finds relevance in the present day. By selecting an era with themes that echo in contemporary society, we bridge the gap between the past and the present, reminding readers that history is a living force that shapes our world today.

In the realm of historical writing, passion and purpose must converge like two rivers meeting at the delta. It is the passion for the chosen era, the eagerness to unearth its mysteries, and the zeal to bring its characters to life that will propel us forward. And in this confluence of passion and purpose, we find the inspiration to navigate the uncharted waters of history and craft stories that captivate the hearts and minds of readers.

The craft of the historical writer is not limited by the compass of fact but is guided by the winds of imagination. The beauty of historical fiction lies in the freedom to reimagine the past, to breathe life into historical figures, and to explore counterfactual scenarios. In the vast expanse of history, the historical writer becomes both cartographer and storyteller, charting the course with a blend of rigorous research and boundless creativity.

As a historical writer, I find myself drawn to the shores of diverse horizons. Each era offers a different landscape, a unique tapestry of cultures, and a myriad of untold stories. It is in the celebration of this diversity that historical fiction truly comes alive. By giving voice to marginalized characters, exploring underrepresented perspectives, and embracing the full spectrum of human experience, we paint a vivid tableau of history's kaleidoscope.

The journey of the historical writer is a never-ending voyage. Each era explored becomes a stepping stone to the next, and the currents of time carry us forward into uncharted territories. As we choose our historical eras, we embark on a quest to unveil the mysteries of the past and illuminate the shadows of history. With every word penned, we navigate the currents of time, ensuring that the stories of the past continue to resonate in the hearts of readers for generations to come.

As a historical fiction writer, choosing the right historical era is a critical decision that will shape the entire trajectory of your novel. The historical era provides the backdrop for your story, influencing the setting, characters, conflicts, and themes. Here are some essential considerations to help you make an informed choice when selecting your historical era:

Start by exploring historical eras that genuinely fascinate and excite you. Your passion for the era will translate into the authenticity and enthusiasm of your writing. Whether it's the intrigue of the ancient world, the romance of the Victorian era, or the turbulence of a particular historical event, your genuine interest will fuel your creativity and drive your commitment to research.

Before settling on an era, evaluate the availability of historical records and resources. Ample historical research material will help you craft a well-rounded and accurate portrayal of the time period. Robust research will also provide you with the necessary context and details to immerse readers in the historical setting.

Consider how your chosen historical era relates to contemporary themes and issues. Historical fiction has the power to shed light on present-day concerns by drawing parallels between the past and the present. Exploring themes such as women's rights, social justice, or the impact of war from a historical perspective can resonate with modern readers and make your story more compelling.

While popular historical eras like medieval Europe or World

War II are rich in material, consider exploring less commonly depicted settings. Uncovering lesser-known or underexplored historical eras can offer a fresh perspective and unique narrative opportunities. This could also give you a chance to bring to life the stories of marginalized communities whose experiences are often overlooked.

Think about the type of characters you envision for your story. Certain historical eras may provide a better fit for specific character archetypes or personality traits. For instance, a daring pirate might thrive in the Golden Age of Piracy, while a progressive suffragette could find her place during the suffrage movement.

Every historical era has its challenges and limitations when it comes to historical accuracy and representation. Be mindful of cultural sensitivity and potential biases while depicting historical events or characters. Strive to avoid anachronisms and cultural misrepresentations to create a respectful and authentic portrayal of the past.

Consider exploring historical eras that involve cross-cultural interactions or international settings. Such narratives can offer a rich tapestry of diverse characters, conflicts, and themes, bringing a global perspective to your historical fiction.

Your chosen historical era can also influence the genre and style of your writing. For example, certain time periods might be better suited to mystery, romance, adventure, or political intrigue. Tailoring your era to your preferred genre can enhance the impact and appeal of your story.

Choosing the right historical era is a pivotal decision for any historical fiction writer. It sets the stage for your storytelling, impacting the authenticity, relevance, and emotional resonance of your narrative. By considering your personal interests, research potential, relevance to contemporary themes, and character compatibility, you can find the perfect historical era to embark on a captivating journey of historical fiction.

Chapter 9

Researching Different Historical Eras

Researching different historical periods is a crucial and exciting aspect of writing historical fiction. The process of delving into the past allows writers to gain a deep understanding of the chosen era, its context, and its people. Through thorough research, historical fiction writers can create authentic and immersive narratives that transport readers to another time. Here, we explore the importance of historical research and provide insights into effective research methods for exploring different historical periods.

The Pillars of Historical Fiction

At the heart of every compelling historical fiction lies meticulous research. Without a strong foundation of historical knowledge, the narrative risks losing its authenticity and credibility. Research serves as the pillars upon which the story is built, supporting the characters, setting, and events in a historically accurate context.

To begin researching a historical period, immerse yourself in the broader historical context. Familiarize yourself with the political, social, and cultural landscape of the time. Learn about the major events, significant figures, and prevailing ideologies that shaped the era.

Reading historical books, academic articles, and primary sources written during or close to the time period can provide invaluable insights. Analyzing art, literature, and music from the era can also offer a window into the mindset and emotions of the people who lived during that time.

Primary sources are firsthand accounts or materials created during the historical period under study. These sources include letters, diaries, official documents, newspapers, and artifacts. They provide a direct link to the past, offering authentic and unfiltered glimpses into the lives of people from that era.

Secondary sources, on the other hand, are interpretations or analyses of primary sources written by historians or scholars. They provide context, analysis, and different perspectives on historical events. Relying on reputable secondary sources enhances the depth and accuracy of your understanding.

Visiting archives and museums can be a treasure trove for historical fiction writers. Many archives house collections of letters, documents, photographs, and other primary sources. Exploring these materials can offer unique insights and specific details that bring your historical narrative to life.

Museums with historical exhibits also provide a tangible experience of the era, allowing you to immerse yourself in the physical artifacts of the time. Viewing historical artifacts in person can evoke a sense of connection to the past, aiding your writing process.

The digital age has made historical research more accessible than ever. Online databases, digital archives, and academic journals provide a wealth of information on different historical periods. Online resources also enable cross-referencing and fact-checking, ensuring the accuracy of your narrative.

Libraries remain essential havens for historical research. Traditional books and scholarly works complement digital resources, offering a vast array of knowledge that can deepen your understanding of the era.

Engaging with experts in the field can be a valuable asset during your research journey. Historians, scholars, and researchers can provide valuable insights, answer specific questions, and offer guidance on lesser-known aspects of the era.

Participating in historical conferences, workshops, or lectures can also enrich your understanding of the historical period. Interacting with fellow enthusiasts and scholars can spark new ideas and perspectives for your narrative.

While research is essential for historical accuracy, it is equally crucial to exercise selective inclusion in your narrative. Not every historical detail needs to be included; instead, prioritize the elements that serve the plot and character development.

Selective inclusion allows you to strike a balance between historical accuracy and the creative liberties required to craft a compelling story. Remember that historical fiction is not a history lesson; it is a work of art that transports readers to another time while evoking emotions and connections.

Researching different historical periods is a journey of time travel. It is an opportunity for historical fiction writers to explore the vast expanse of human history, connecting with the people and events that shaped our world.

The process of research is as vital as the act of writing itself. It enriches your understanding, inspires your creativity, and enhances the authenticity of your narrative. As you embark on this journey of discovery, remember that historical research is not a task to be rushed; rather, it is an immersive and transformative experience that will shape your historical fiction into a vivid and captivating portrayal of the past.

Chapter 10

Selecting an Era That Resonates with You

As a historical fiction writer, selecting a historical era to write about is a deeply personal and resonant decision. The era you choose becomes the canvas on which you paint your narrative, and it is essential to choose one that ignites your passion and sparks your creativity. Here are some considerations to help you select a historical era that truly resonates with you:

1. Personal Interest and Fascination: Begin by exploring your own interests and passions. Reflect on the historical periods that have always fascinated you, the events that have captured your imagination, or the figures whose stories have intrigued you. Writing about an era that genuinely interests you will infuse your narrative with authenticity and enthusiasm.

2. Emotional Connection: Consider the historical periods that evoke strong emotions within you. An era that elicits a visceral response can serve as a powerful foundation for your writing. Emotionally connecting to the era will fuel your commitment to research and storytelling, resulting in a more compelling narrative.

3. Themes and Relevance: Explore the themes from historical eras that resonate with contemporary issues. Look for connections between the past and the present, and consider how the era you choose can provide insights into current societal, political, or cultural challenges.

4. Historical Significance: Evaluate the historical significance of the era you are interested in. An era with pivotal events, transformative movements, or influential figures can offer a rich backdrop for storytelling and provide ample material for research.

5. Marginalized Voices and Untold Stories: Seek out historical eras that give you the opportunity to highlight marginalized voices or untold stories. Writing about individuals or communities whose narratives have been overlooked by traditional history can be a powerful way to reclaim lost narratives and promote inclusivity in historical fiction.

6. Diversity of Characters and Perspectives: Consider how the historical era allows you to explore a diverse range of characters and perspectives. An era with a wide array of social, cultural, and ethnic backgrounds can enrich your narrative and offer opportunities for engaging storytelling.

7. Challenges and Growth: Choose an era that presents intellectual and creative challenges for you as a writer. Writing historical fiction requires rigorous research and imaginative interpretation. Embracing the complexities of the era will lead to personal growth as a writer and storyteller.

8. Setting and Atmosphere: The setting and atmosphere of the historical era should also resonate with you. Visualize the landscapes, cultures, and environments of the past and consider how they align with your creative vision.

9. Genre Compatibility: Different historical eras may align better with specific sub-genres of historical fiction, such as romance, mystery, adventure, or political intrigue. Consider how your chosen era complements the genre you wish to explore.

10. Connection to Characters: Finally, envision the characters that might inhabit the historical era you are considering. Allow yourself to connect with them on a personal level and envision their stories coming to life through your writing.

Ultimately, the historical era you choose to write about should be one that excites, inspires, and moves you. Trust your instincts and follow the call of history's winds as you embark on a journey of research, imagination, and storytelling. Your passion for the era will infuse your writing with authenticity, and your enthusiasm will carry readers on a captivating voyage through time.

Balancing accuracy and creative freedom in writing historical fiction is a delicate task that requires a thoughtful approach. Striking the right balance between these two elements is essential to create a compelling and engaging story while still respecting the historical context. Here are some tips to help you navigate this balance:

1. **Research Thoroughly**: Immersing yourself in the historical period you're writing about is crucial. Research the time, place, culture, social norms, and major events. Read primary sources, scholarly works, and accounts from the era. This foundation will enable you to create a believable setting for your story.

2. **Respect the Historical Record**: While you have creative freedom, it's important to respect the fundamental historical facts. Major events, key figures, and significant societal norms should be accurate. Altering these too drastically can lead to a loss of authenticity and may alienate readers who appreciate historical accuracy.

3. **Identify Gaps**: Historical records can have gaps, particularly regarding everyday life, personal interactions, and lesser-known figures. This is where

your creative freedom can shine. Fill in these gaps with well-reasoned conjecture, but always ensure your speculations align with what is known and plausible for the time period.

4. **Create Believable Characters**: Your characters should feel authentic to the era, both in terms of their behavior and their beliefs. They can hold attitudes that were common at the time, but be cautious not to present anything that feels anachronistic or overly modern.

5. **Establish a Historical Tone**: Use language, dialogue, and descriptions that evoke the period you're writing about. This can help transport readers to that time and make the story more immersive.

6. **Acknowledge Artistic License**: In an author's note or preface, you can explicitly mention where you've taken creative liberties. This acknowledgment can help readers understand that while you've stayed true to the historical essence, you've exercised creative freedom in certain areas.

7. **Beta Readers and Historical Experts**: Have beta readers who are well-versed in the historical period you're depicting. They can provide valuable feedback on the historical accuracy and the overall feeling of the story. If possible, consult with historical experts to ensure your portrayal aligns with the accepted understanding of the time.

8. **Revise and Refine**: After weaving your creative elements into the historical framework, revise your work meticulously. Ensure that the creative aspects enhance the story without detracting from the historical integrity.

Balancing accuracy and creative freedom is a skill that improves with practice. By respecting the historical record while exploring the imaginative possibilities, you can create historical fiction that captivates readers while honoring the past.

Chapter 11
What Ernest Hemingway Teaches About Crafting Believable Characters

Ernest Hemingway, the iconic American author, is renowned for his succinct prose, strong characters, and ability to capture the essence of human nature. His approach to creating believable characters in fiction offers valuable lessons for writers seeking to imbue their own stories with authenticity and depth.

Hemingway's writing is often characterized by its economy of words and emphasis on showing rather than telling. This principle applies directly to character development. Instead of explicitly stating a character's traits, let their actions, dialogue, and interactions reveal who they are.

Consider "The Old Man and the Sea." Santiago, the aging fisherman, is not described in a laundry list of adjectives. Instead, his character shines through his determination, resilience, and the way he talks about the sea. This approach invites readers to form their own impressions of Santiago, making him a more vivid and believable character.

Hemingway's dialogue is a masterclass in subtext. Characters often say less than what they mean, and their true feelings are hidden beneath the surface. This creates a sense of realism, as people in real life rarely express everything openly.

In "Hills Like White Elephants," the central conflict is subtly conveyed through a conversation between a man and a woman in a train station. Hemingway's sparse dialogue leaves much unsaid, allowing readers to infer the depth of their relationship and the weight of the decision they face. This technique adds layers to the characters and encourages readers to engage with the story on a deeper level.

Believable characters have clear motivations that drive their actions. Hemingway's characters are often driven by fundamental desires and conflicts that resonate with universal human experiences.

In "For Whom the Bell Tolls," the protagonist, Robert Jordan, is motivated by his commitment to a cause he believes in and his love for Maria. These driving forces shape his decisions and actions throughout the novel. Understanding the core motivations of your characters allows you to create authentic, relatable individuals.

Hemingway's characters are not flawless heroes; they have vulnerabilities and imperfections that make them human. Flaws add depth and complexity to characters, making them more believable and relatable.

Take Jake Barnes from "The Sun Also Rises." He is a war veteran dealing with impotence, which adds a layer of vulnerability to his character. This vulnerability makes him more compelling and allows readers to empathize with his struggles. Embracing your characters' flaws can lead to richer, more authentic portrayals.

Characters don't exist in a vacuum; their environment and the historical context in which they live significantly impact their beliefs, actions, and relationships. Hemingway's characters are deeply influenced by their surroundings, and understanding this context is essential for creating believable characters.

In "A Farewell to Arms," the World War I setting deeply

affects the characters' experiences and choices. The war shapes their perspectives on love, life, and death. Incorporating the historical, cultural, and societal context of your story enriches your characters and makes their actions more plausible within that framework.

Hemingway's exploration of universal themes contributes to the timeless appeal of his characters. Love, loss, courage, and the human struggle are themes that transcend time and resonate with readers across generations.

In "The Old Man and the Sea," the themes of perseverance, the connection between man and nature, and the resilience of the human spirit make Santiago's character compelling to readers of all ages. Crafting characters whose experiences and emotions tap into these universal themes helps create a lasting impact on your audience.

Hemingway's spare and precise descriptions contribute to the vividness of his characters. He selects details that are essential, painting a clear picture without overwhelming the reader with unnecessary information.

In "The Short Happy Life of Francis Macomber," Hemingway's economical description of Francis Macomber's physical appearance hints at his weakness and contrasts it with his wife's confidence. This brief but impactful description gives readers a vivid impression of Macomber's character. Practicing the art of selecting meaningful details can make your characters more memorable and believable.

The dynamics between characters are a fertile ground for character development. Hemingway's characters often engage in complex relationships that reveal aspects of their personalities and drive the plot forward.

In "A Moveable Feast," Hemingway's memoir of his time in Paris, his interactions with fellow writers like F. Scott

Fitzgerald and Gertrude Stein provide insight into his own character and the challenges he faced. Exploring the relationships between your characters—whether they're friends, enemies, or lovers—can unveil layers of their identities and motivations.

Ernest Hemingway's approach to creating believable characters emphasizes the power of showing over telling, the importance of subtext, the significance of motivations, the value of embracing flaws, the impact of context, the resonance of universal themes, the art of economical description, and the exploration of relationships. By incorporating these insights into your writing, you can craft characters that come alive on the page, engaging your readers and immersing them in the world you've created. Hemingway's legacy serves as a timeless guide for writers aspiring to breathe authenticity and depth into their fictional characters.

Chapter 12
Weaving Authenticity into Fictional Worlds

Historical fiction is a captivating genre that allows readers to journey into the past, immersing themselves in bygone eras, cultures, and events. Yet, this genre presents a unique challenge for writers: how to balance the allure of an imaginative narrative with the demand for historical accuracy; the intricate dance between historical accuracy and character development, revealing how these two elements intertwine to create rich, believable, and captivating stories.

The Power of Historical Accuracy

When we speak of historical accuracy, we refer to the fidelity of a narrative to the historical facts, events, and societal norms of the time period in which it is set. It's the art of recreating the past with precision, allowing readers to step back in time and experience the world as it truly was. The importance of historical accuracy cannot be overstated, as it forms the foundation upon which all other elements of the story rest.

Imagine a novel set in medieval Europe. The historical accuracy of this setting, complete with accurate descriptions of castles, clothing, and daily life, forms the canvas on which your characters will be painted. It lends credibility to the narrative and invites readers to fully invest in the world you've created.

Historical accuracy adds depth and texture to the setting, creating an immersive experience. Whether it's the cobblestone streets of a Renaissance city or the rugged landscapes of the American Wild West, the accuracy of these details not only paints a vivid picture but also shapes the characters' experiences and interactions.

Historical accuracy introduces unique challenges and conflicts that can drive the plot forward. It can be the political turmoil of a revolution, the social constraints of a particular era, or the technological limitations of the time. These historical elements create a dynamic backdrop against which your characters must navigate.

Consider a story set during World War II. The historical accuracy of the war's impact on society—rationing, fear, sacrifice—adds a layer of tension to the characters' lives. It forces them to make difficult choices, endure hardships, and adapt to the ever-changing circumstances. This conflict is born from historical accuracy and becomes an integral part of character development.

Accurate historical context opens the door to exploring the complexities of human nature within the framework of a specific time period. It allows writers to delve into the attitudes, beliefs, and social norms that prevailed during that era, providing a window into the motivations and struggles of their characters.

For example, a character living in ancient Greece may grapple with the philosophical debates of the time, such as the clash between reason and mythology. This intellectual struggle, rooted in historical accuracy, shapes the character's worldview, aspirations, and conflicts, driving their development in a way that resonates with the period.

Historical accuracy can foster empathy by immersing readers in the lives of characters who faced challenges and triumphs in a very different world. By understanding the historical context, readers can appreciate the struggles characters endure, empathize with their decisions, and gain a deeper understanding of the human experience throughout history.

For instance, a story set during the Great Depression might follow a family as they navigate unemployment and economic hardship. By experiencing these challenges alongside the characters, readers gain insights into the resilience and resourcefulness required to survive during that era.

The Crucial Role of Character Development

While historical accuracy provides the framework, it is the characters who breathe life into the narrative. They are the vessels through which readers experience the historical context, and their growth, transformation, and relationships are what ultimately drive the emotional resonance of the story.

Characters must be true to the time period in which they exist. They should embody the values, beliefs, and behaviors that were prevalent during that era. This authenticity not only enhances the historical accuracy of the narrative but also creates characters who are deeply embedded in their cultural and societal context.

Imagine a novel set in ancient Egypt. The characters' beliefs in the pantheon of gods, their adherence to social hierarchies, and their daily routines must reflect the historical realities of that civilization. This alignment between characters and historical accuracy creates a seamless integration that enhances the overall believability of the story.

Historical accuracy can serve as a catalyst for character development. The challenges and opportunities presented by the historical context force characters to evolve, adapt, and grow. As they confront the realities of their time, they may question their beliefs, face moral dilemmas, or undergo personal transformations that resonate with readers.

Consider a character living during the suffrage movement. As she becomes increasingly involved in the fight for women's rights, her journey from uncertainty to empowerment mirrors the broader historical shift. This connection between her personal development and the historical events adds depth to both her character arc and the overall narrative.

As stated before and worth repeating: Characters don't exist in a vacuum; they are shaped by the historical events that surround them. Conversely, characters can also influence the course of history within the confines of your fictional world. This dynamic interplay between characters and their historical context creates a vibrant and engaging narrative.

In a story set during the Renaissance, a character's innovative ideas and artistic pursuits may contribute to the cultural shifts of that time. By weaving their actions into the historical tapestry, you create a sense of agency for your characters, making them active participants in the larger historical narrative.

Ultimately, it is through characters that readers connect emotionally with the past. By experiencing the joys, sorrows, triumphs, and failures of characters living in a different time, readers develop a profound connection to history. This connection transcends facts and dates, allowing readers to empathize with the individuals who inhabited that era.

A novel set during the Civil Rights Movement can introduce readers to characters who grapple with the injustices and inequalities of that time. By walking in the shoes of these characters, readers gain a visceral understanding of the struggles faced by individuals during that pivotal period in history.

Historical accuracy and character development are not

opposing forces; they are partners in the creation of a compelling historical fiction narrative. Together, they form a harmonious dance where the authenticity of the past enhances the depth of the characters, and the characters, in turn, breathe life into the historical backdrop.

The journey toward historical accuracy begins with thorough research. Dive into primary sources, immerse yourself in the details of the time period, and understand the nuances of the culture, politics, and daily life. This research becomes the foundation on which you build your characters' world.

For example, if you're writing a story set in ancient Rome, study not only the major historical events but also the customs, social classes, and technological advancements of that era. These details will seep into your characters' lives, shaping their experiences and interactions.

While characters must be true to their historical context, they should also be individuals with unique personalities, motivations, and arcs. Don't reduce them to mere representatives of their time; instead, allow them to shine as distinct individuals who respond to the historical challenges in ways that reveal their inner complexities.

A character in a story set during the Industrial Revolution might possess personal ambitions that go against the societal norms of the time. Perhaps she dreams of becoming an engineer in a male-dominated field. This individual aspiration, in the face of historical constraints, adds depth to her character and makes her relatable to readers.

The interaction between characters, both with each other and with the historical context, generates conflict, tension, and growth. Characters can challenge societal norms, confront authority, or collaborate to overcome the obstacles of their time.

In a story set during the Renaissance, the clash of ideas between characters—artists, thinkers, and traditionalists—can drive the plot. This clash not only reflects the intellectual ferment of the period but also creates a fertile ground for character development as they grapple with differing worldviews.

Character development within the framework of historical accuracy should be meaningful and resonant. Characters should learn, evolve, and adapt in ways that reflect the impact of their historical experiences. These transformations, whether subtle or profound, allow readers to witness the growth of characters and their response to the changing world around them.

In a story set during the Enlightenment, a character's transition from blind adherence to tradition to a more rational and open-minded perspective aligns with the intellectual currents of the time. This evolution serves as both a personal journey and a reflection of the broader historical movement.

The delicate balance between historical accuracy and character development is the key to crafting a successful historical fiction narrative. Neither element should overshadow the other. Instead, they should complement and enrich each other, creating a cohesive and immersive reading experience.

As you write, constantly evaluate the interplay between historical accuracy and character development. Does the historical context enhance the characters' experiences and choices? Does the characters' growth align with the challenges and opportunities presented by the historical period? Strive for a seamless integration where both elements work in harmony.

Historical accuracy and character development are inseparable threads in the tapestry of historical fiction. The authenticity of the past provides the canvas, while the characters breathe life and emotion into the narrative. The interplay between these elements creates a compelling and immersive experience for readers, allowing them to not only learn about history but also to feel it through the eyes of characters who lived, loved, and struggled in a world that now exists within the pages of a book. Balancing historical accuracy and character development is a challenging endeavor, but when executed with skill and sensitivity, it results in stories that transport readers across time, enrich their understanding of the human experience, and leave a lasting impact on their hearts and minds.

Chapter 13
Blending Fictional and Historical Characters:
Creating a Harmonious Tapestry

One of the most intriguing aspects of this genre is the interplay between fictional and historical characters. When done skillfully, blending these characters creates a harmonious tapestry that enhances the authenticity of the historical setting while adding depth and relatability to the story.

The Power of Historical Characters

Historical characters, based on real individuals who lived during a specific time period, bring an air of authenticity to historical fiction. They can be renowned figures, such as historical leaders, artists, or explorers, or lesser-known individuals whose experiences provide unique perspectives on the era in question. Including historical characters in your story offers several advantages:

Historical characters act as touchstones, grounding the narrative in the historical period you wish to explore. They provide readers with recognizable figures, familiar names from textbooks or historical accounts, which immediately transport them to the era you're depicting.

For example, if you're writing a novel set during the American Revolution, featuring figures like George Washington, Benjamin Franklin, or Thomas Jefferson immediately establishes the time frame. Readers connect with these historical giants, allowing you to build the world around them.

Through the eyes of historical characters, readers gain insights into the major events, social dynamics, and cultural norms of the time. These characters can act as conduits, allowing readers to witness historical moments from a more personal perspective.

Suppose your story involves a young woman living in Renaissance Italy. Her interactions with a renowned artist of the time, like Leonardo da Vinci, can provide a window into the artistic and intellectual ferment of that period. Her experiences become a microcosm of the broader historical context, allowing readers to engage with the era on a personal level.

Historical characters, just like their fictional counterparts, can be catalysts for conflict and change within the narrative. Their goals, actions, and interactions with other characters can drive the plot forward, creating tension and opportunities for growth.

Consider a novel set during the Civil War, where a protagonist interacts with historical figures like Abraham Lincoln or Harriet Tubman. These interactions can spark important decisions, moral dilemmas, or unexpected alliances, propelling the story in directions that resonate with the historical events of that time.

The Richness of Fictional Characters

While historical characters bring authenticity, fictional characters add versatility, allowing writers to explore a wider range of perspectives, experiences, and emotions. Fictional characters are the conduits through which readers experience the historical world, and they serve as a means of injecting personal narratives into the broader historical landscape. Here are the advantages of including fictional characters in a historical setting:

Fictional characters often represent the ordinary individuals who lived during the historical period, offering readers a relatable perspective. These characters can come from various social backgrounds, occupations, or walks of life, enabling you to explore the experiences of everyday people during that era.

For instance, in a story set during the Industrial Revolution, a factory worker struggling to make ends meet may embody the challenges faced by the working class, giving readers a glimpse into the socioeconomic disparities of that time.

Fictional characters allow writers to craft unique personal stories within the historical framework. Through these characters, you can explore themes of love, friendship, ambition, and adversity that resonate universally, transcending the specifics of the historical period.

Imagine a tale set in ancient Rome, where a young slave dreams of freedom. This fictional character's journey, filled with trials and triumphs, becomes a compelling narrative thread that draws readers in, even as it reveals the complexities of Roman society.

Fictional characters provide the flexibility to shape the narrative according to your creative vision. While historical characters come with established biographies and known actions, fictional characters offer a blank canvas, allowing you to guide their arcs, choices, and relationships in ways that serve your storytelling goals.

For example, if your story is set during the Renaissance, a fictional artist struggling to gain recognition may interact with historical figures like Michelangelo or Raphael. The interactions between the fictional artist and these real-life luminaries can add depth to the narrative, while the fictional character's personal journey remains under your creative control.

The Art of Blending: Techniques and Challenges

Blending historical and fictional characters requires a delicate balance, with each character type enriching the other to create a seamless and engaging narrative. Here are techniques that writers use to master this art, along with the challenges they must navigate:

A solid understanding of the historical period is crucial for integrating historical and fictional characters seamlessly. Research not only the major historical events but also the smaller details of daily life, social hierarchies, language, and cultural norms.

When blending a fictional character with historical figures like Henry VIII's court, you must ensure that the fictional character's background and interactions align with the historical accuracy of the Tudor era. This research-based foundation lends credibility to the character's presence in that world.

Interactions between historical and fictional characters must feel authentic, with each character's actions and dialogue reflecting the time period and their respective backgrounds.

If your story features a fictional soldier in World War I interacting with historical figures like Winston Churchill or T.E. Lawrence, the conversations, attitudes, and reactions of these characters should be consistent with the realities of the war and the personalities of the historical figures involved.

Every character, historical or fictional, should serve the larger narrative. Each character should have clear motivations, goals, and arcs that contribute to the plot's development.

If your story revolves around a young woman during the Salem witch trials who interacts with both historical figures and fictional townspeople, each character's role in the unfolding events should drive the story forward, revealing different facets of the historical period and enhancing the overall thematic exploration.

Striking the right balance between historical and fictional characters is essential. While historical characters bring authenticity, fictional characters provide a personal connection for readers. Ensure that the narrative doesn't become overshadowed by the historical figures or, conversely, overly reliant on the fictional characters.

In a story set during the French Revolution, where a fictional commoner interacts with historical figures like Marie Antoinette or Maximilien Robespierre, the focus should remain on the fictional character's experiences and how they intersect with the broader historical events, allowing readers to connect on a personal level while appreciating the historical backdrop.

A unifying theme or central question can tie together the experiences of both historical and fictional characters, creating a cohesive narrative. This theme could be a moral dilemma, a quest for justice, or the pursuit of a shared goal.

In a story set during the Harlem Renaissance, a fictional jazz musician rubbing shoulders with historical figures like Langston Hughes or Duke Ellington might explore the theme of artistic expression as a form of resistance and empowerment, a theme that resonates with both the fictional and historical characters' experiences.

Blending fictional and historical characters is an art that enhances the richness of historical fiction. Historical characters provide authenticity, allowing readers to connect with recognizable figures from the past, while fictional characters bring personal narratives that resonate universally. The interplay between these character types creates a tapestry where the historical setting comes alive through the eyes of relatable individuals.

As a writer, embracing the challenges and opportunities of blending these characters can elevate your historical fiction, transporting readers to a different time, engaging them with personal stories, and illuminating the complexities of the human experience across the ages. When historical and fictional characters unite in a harmonious narrative, the result is a powerful and immersive journey that bridges the gap between history and imagination, leaving a lasting impact on readers' hearts and minds.

Chapter 14
Unveiling the Heart of the Past:
Developing Character Motivations
in Historical Context

In the realm of historical fiction, where the past and imagination intertwine, character motivations serve as the lifeblood of a compelling narrative. These motivations propel characters through the tumultuous currents of history, offering readers a window into the human experiences of bygone eras.

The Crucial Role of Character Motivations

Character motivations are the driving forces that guide a character's actions, decisions, and desires throughout a story. These motivations spring from a character's wants, needs, fears, and aspirations, and they shape the choices they make, the conflicts they face, and the growth they undergo. When set against the backdrop of a historical context, character motivations gain added layers of depth and meaning.

In historical fiction, character motivations must harmonize with the historical period in which they exist. The beliefs, values, and societal norms of that time frame should influence a character's internal landscape, driving their hopes and fears in ways that resonate with the era.

Consider a character living during the Elizabethan era, a time marked by political intrigue and religious upheaval. Their motivations might be colored by loyalty to the monarchy, the desire for advancement at court, or the pursuit of religious freedom. These motivations echo the tensions and priorities of the time, enhancing the character's authenticity.

Character motivations offer writers an avenue to explore the complexities of history through personal experiences. By delving into characters' desires and dilemmas, writers can illuminate lesser-known aspects of a historical period, shedding light on the everyday lives of individuals who lived through significant events.

For instance, a character's motivation to join a suffrage movement during the Progressive Era allows readers to understand the challenges faced by women seeking equality. Through this character's journey, the broader historical context becomes intimate and relatable.

Character motivations often collide with external challenges, leading to internal and external conflicts. Historical contexts provide unique obstacles and dilemmas that can heighten the stakes and intensify the conflicts characters face.

In a story set during the American Civil War, a character's motivations to uphold their family's honor may clash with their growing disillusionment with the war's violence and injustice. This inner turmoil, informed by both personal values and historical circumstances, deepens the character's arc and resonates with readers. A stellar example of this is portrayed in Frazier's *Cold Mountain.*

Historical contexts are characterized by change—social, political, and cultural transformations that impact individuals and societies. Characters' motivations can serve as a lens through which readers witness these changes, allowing them to observe the evolution of values, attitudes, and aspirations over time.

Imagine a character living through the Roaring Twenties, a period of societal shifts and changing norms. Their motivations to break free from traditional roles and seek personal fulfillment might embody the spirit of the era, reflecting both their personal desires and the larger cultural changes. Jay Gatsby's personal desires and motivations propel the story told by Fitzgerald and is a noteworthy novel for any historial novelist to study when learning about character motivation.

Strategies for Crafting Historical Motivations

Developing character motivations within a historical context requires a delicate interplay of research, empathy, and narrative craftsmanship. Here are strategies that writers employ to create resonant and authentic character motivations:

Thorough research is the cornerstone of crafting character motivations in historical contexts. Immerse yourself in the time period, studying primary sources, historical accounts, and cultural nuances. This research provides the raw materials for constructing motivations that are rooted in the era's realities.

If your story is set during the Victorian era, explore the societal expectations placed on women, the prevailing attitudes toward class and gender, and the impact of industrialization. These historical insights will inform the motivations and choices of your characters, making them credible products of their time.

Character motivations should align with the cultural norms and values of the historical period. These norms shape characters' goals, fears, and aspirations, influencing the choices they make and the conflicts they encounter.

In a story set during the Renaissance, a character's motivation to gain recognition as an artist might be shaped by the prevailing emphasis on creativity and innovation. Understanding the cultural reverence for art during this period helps ground the character's aspirations in the historical ethos.

Just as individuals in the present have multifaceted motivations, characters in historical contexts should embody complexity. Embrace the ambiguity of human nature, allowing characters to have conflicting motivations that reflect the contradictions of their time.

For example, a character in a story set during the French Revolution might be torn between their loyalty to the monarchy and their growing sympathy for the revolutionary cause. This internal conflict mirrors the uncertainties of the era and adds depth to the character's journey.

While characters' motivations should be informed by their historical setting, they should also resonate on a universal level. By connecting characters' desires to universal themes such as love, freedom, justice, and identity, you create emotional entry points for readers across time.

In a story set during the Civil Rights Movement, a character's motivation to fight against racial inequality aligns with the larger historical struggle, while also speaking to the timeless theme of justice and equality.

Characters are not solely influenced by their historical context; personal experiences, relationships, and individual values also shape their motivations. Blend these layers of influence to create multi-dimensional characters who respond to history in unique ways.

For instance, a character in a story set during World War II might have motivations rooted in their family's history of military service, their personal connections to soldiers, and their patriotic ideals. These varied influences create a rich tapestry of motivations that enrich the character's journey.

Developing character motivations within a historical context is a delicate dance that requires a deep understanding of both the past and the human psyche. By melding historical realities with characters' desires, fears, and aspirations, writers craft narratives that resonate on multiple levels. These characters become not just vessels for historical exploration, but windows through which readers witness the joys, sorrows, and complexities of individuals who lived in different times.

In the realm of historical fiction, character motivations are the bridge that connects readers to history, inviting them to empathize, understand, and reflect on the human experiences that transcend time. When woven into the fabric of historical contexts, these motivations elevate characters from mere ink on a page to living embodiments of the past, leaving an indelible mark on the readers who journey into your story.

Chapter 15

J.R.R. Tolkien's Legacy: A Masterclass in World-Building and Authentic Setting Creation

In the realm of speculative fiction, few names resonate as profoundly as J.R.R. Tolkien. His monumental works, "The Hobbit" and "The Lord of the Rings" trilogy, not only captivated generations of readers but also revolutionized the art of world-building and setting creation in fiction. Tolkien's meticulous craftsmanship, attention to detail, and boundless imagination crafted immersive and authentic fictional realms. By delving into the lessons Tolkien can teach writers about world-building and creating an authentic setting, authors can explore the techniques, philosophy, and enduring impact of his approach in relation to utilizing some of the same physics on their own writing.

The Art of World-Building

In the days of yore, when the realms of historical fiction stretched forth like uncharted lands waiting to be explored, there lived a tradition, a noble craft, akin to the art of the loremasters who wove tales of Middle-earth. This craft, known as world-building, was not limited to fantastical realms but extended its roots into the annals of history, unearthing the treasures of bygone eras, forging the tapestries of long-forgotten epochs, and revealing the grandeur and intricacies of the past.

Just as the ancient sages of the Shire mapped the paths and valleys of their beloved land, so too do the creators of historical fiction embark on a quest to chart the contours of distant ages. They venture forth with quill in hand, seeking to recreate the lost realms, to breathe life into those who trod the earth when the world was yet young. The heart of historical fiction beats with the pulse of the past, resonating with the echoes of history, and it is in the art of world-building that this heartbeat finds its rhythm.

In the realm of historical fiction, the terrain is not a canvas blank and waiting for the artist's brush; it is a palimpsest, layered with the footprints of generations, etched with the events, cultures, and beliefs that once shaped the course of the world. The world-builder must be a scholar, a historian, a custodian of the past. They delve into dusty tomes, decipher ancient scrolls, and immerse themselves in the chronicles of times long gone. They seek the truth, not of the fantastical, but of the tangible, for historical fiction finds its magic in authenticity.

Behold the foundations of this craft, the pillars upon which the world-builder's work stands:

Research, the Backbone: The historian's art is as crucial to the world-builder as a sturdy foundation to a fortress. In the historical fiction realm, every detail must be carefully excavated from the annals of history. From the sprawling empires to the tiniest hamlets, from the customs and traditions to the battles fought in forgotten fields, the world-builder's research is an unending quest for the truth of the past.

As the loremasters of old sifted through the lore of elves and dwarves, so too does the historical world-builder immerse themselves in historical accounts, eyewitness testimonies, and the artifacts left behind by those who walked the earth centuries before. The goal is not mere replication, but understanding, for it is only through deep understanding that the world-builder can craft a setting that resonates with the echoes of history.

Detail, the Weaving of Threads: Just as a master weaver spins threads of different colors to create a tapestry, the historical world-builder weaves together myriad details to construct a vibrant and authentic setting. Every aspect, from the garments worn by the inhabitants to the food on their tables, from the architecture of their dwellings to the language they speak, contributes to the rich tapestry of the past.

In the realm of historical fiction, the smallest details matter, for they paint a vivid picture of the world, drawing readers into its embrace. A character's mannerisms, a street vendor's wares, the aroma of a bustling market, all these elements converge to create a sense of immersion. The historical world-builder is not a mere storyteller; they are a time-traveler, transporting readers to eras long gone, allowing them to experience the past in all its splendor and complexity.

Authenticity, the Soul of the Past: The hallmark of historical fiction is authenticity. The world-builder must strive for a faithful representation of the past, capturing the spirit of the era, the beliefs, the social norms, and the challenges faced by those who lived in that age. Just as the creators of Middle-earth imbued their realm with a sense of reality, the historical world-builder must breathe life into their setting by infusing it with the authenticity that comes from a deep understanding of the past.

The characters who traverse this historical landscape must bear the weight of their time, grapple with its trials, and navigate its triumphs. Their motivations, desires, and struggles must be rooted in the historical context, and their interactions with the world around them should reflect the values and challenges of their era.

Imagination, the Bridge to the Past: While the foundation of historical fiction rests upon the bedrock of historical accuracy, the world-builder's imagination is the bridge that connects the past to the present. Just as Tolkien wove myths and legends into the fabric of Middle-earth, the historical world-builder must breathe life into the historical record, infusing it with the vitality that comes from creative interpretation.

The gaps in historical accounts, the mysteries left unanswered by time, these are the canvases upon which the world-builder paints their imaginative strokes. The stories that emerge from these gaps, the characters who emerge from the shadows of history, they become the conduits through which readers experience the past, not as a distant and faded memory, but as a vibrant and living world.

A Sense of Time, the River of Ages: In the heart of historical fiction flows the river of time, carrying the events of the past into the present. The world-builder must embrace this river, understanding that the setting is not a static backdrop but a dynamic stage upon which the forces of history unfold. Kingdoms rise and fall, empires crumble, revolutions ignite, and societies evolve, all within the embrace of the river of time.

As the loremasters of Middle-earth knew that the Ages shaped the destiny of their realm, so too must the historical world-builder recognize the impact of time on their setting. Characters are not isolated entities; they are products of their era, influenced by the events that shaped the world around them. By acknowledging the passage of time, the world-builder adds depth and resonance to the setting, allowing readers to witness the ebb and flow of history.

The Legacy of the Historical World-Builder

In the grand tapestry of literary creation, the historical world-builder is a guardian of the past, a seeker of truths, and a conjurer of realms long faded from the world's memory. Just as the bards of old sang of heroes and legends, the historical world-builder weaves tales of long-lost civilizations, of the ordinary and the extraordinary, of the struggles and triumphs that define the human experience across the ages.

Chapter 16
Immersing Readers in the Past

In the realm of historical fiction, the past beckons like a portal, an intricate tapestry of bygone days woven with the threads of memory and the whispers of history. It is the duty of the storyteller to be not merely a narrator but a time-traveler, a guide who leads readers on a journey across the centuries, immersing them in the rich tapestry of another era, allowing them to walk hand in hand with the ghosts of those who once walked the earth.

The art of immersing readers in the past is a delicate dance, a symphony of words and sensations that transports them beyond the boundaries of the present. Here, the author's pen becomes a magic wand, conjuring not spells but entire worlds, evoking the sights, sounds, smells, and emotions of a time long gone. It is a tapestry woven not with mere threads, but with the vivid threads of imagination and the warp and weft of historical truth.

The Power of Vivid Description: To immerse readers in the past, the writer must wield the power of vivid description. Every scene must be painted with strokes so rich and detailed that readers feel as if they can touch the cobblestones of medieval streets, smell the aroma of spices in a bustling marketplace, and hear the distant echoes of cannon fire during a revolution.

The descriptions should be sensorial, engaging not just the visual sense, but also invoking the other senses. The crunch of autumn leaves underfoot, the taste of salt in the sea breeze, the whisper of silk against skin—the richness of these details creates a multi-dimensional experience that places the reader right in the heart of the historical setting.

Character as a Window: In historical fiction, characters are not mere players on a stage; they are windows through which readers peer into the past. The characters' thoughts, beliefs, and reactions are a mirror reflecting the values, hopes, fears, and challenges of the era in which they live. By crafting characters whose motivations are shaped by the historical context, writers create a bridge that connects readers to the past on an intimate, emotional level.

A character's inner struggles, dilemmas, and personal growth should be inextricably linked to the historical forces at play. As they navigate the challenges of their time, readers gain insight into the larger currents of history that shaped those challenges. Through the characters, readers not only learn about history, but they also experience it, feeling the weight of the past as if it were their own.

Cultural Nuances and Authenticity: Cultural nuances serve as the color palette of the historical canvas, adding depth and authenticity to the setting. Just as every brushstroke contributes to a masterpiece, every cultural detail—the way people greet each other, the customs they follow, the beliefs they hold dear—creates a more immersive experience for readers.

Authenticity is the cornerstone of historical immersion. The writer must become a scholar of the era, delving into the social norms, language, dress, and even the slang of the time. The words on the page should evoke not just the historical period, but the essence of that period, transporting readers to a world where the rhythms of life beat to a different tune.

Dialogue as a Time Machine: Dialogue in historical fiction is a time machine, carrying readers back to a world where the language danced to a different cadence. The way characters speak, the idioms they use, the subtleties of their conversations—all of these contribute to the authenticity of the setting.

The dialogue should not only reflect the language of the era but also convey the beliefs, hierarchies, and power dynamics of the time. The language choices must be consistent with the social strata and the characters' backgrounds, creating a seamless blend of historical accuracy and narrative flow. Through dialogue, readers become not just observers but participants in the conversations of another age.

Exploration of Themes: The past is not just a backdrop; it is a stage for exploring timeless themes. Just as characters confront personal dilemmas, they also grapple with larger questions and ideals that resonate across the ages. By weaving these themes into the narrative, writers create a bridge that allows readers to connect their own lives to the historical context.

Themes of love, courage, justice, and sacrifice, when intertwined with the historical backdrop, become vehicles for deeper exploration. Readers see how these themes manifest in different eras, how they shape characters' choices, and how they transcend time, leaving a mark on the human experience. The historical setting amplifies the resonance of these themes, giving them a weight and depth that linger long after the last page is turned.

Emotional Resonance: The heart of historical fiction lies in its ability to evoke emotions that span centuries. The writer must tap into the emotional reservoir of the era, understanding the hopes, fears, joys, and sorrows that filled the hearts of those who lived in that time. By infusing the narrative with these emotions, writers create a bond between readers and the characters, a bond that transcends time and space.

Whether it's the exhilaration of a battle won, the heartache of a love lost, or the triumph of a hard-fought victory, the emotions of historical characters must resonate with the reader's own humanity. The writer becomes a conduit, channeling the emotional essence of the past, making it palpable and relatable.

The Timeless Spell of Historical Immersion

In the tapestry of literature, historical fiction weaves a spell that transports readers across the chasm of time, allowing them to walk alongside characters whose lives unfolded in eras long gone. Through the power of vivid description, the window of character, the brushstroke of cultural authenticity, the dialogue of another age, the exploration of timeless themes, and the resonance of emotions, the historical fiction writer casts a spell that immerses readers in the past.

Just as a skilled bard weaves tales of old to captivate the hearts of listeners, the historical fiction writer crafts stories that resonate with the human experience, bridging the gap between past and present, and leaving an indelible mark on the souls of those who embark on the journey. The past, once distant and forgotten, becomes alive, tangible, and eternally relevant, a testament to the power of historical immersion in the hands of a master storyteller.

Chapter 17
Researching Locations and Settings

In the realm of historical fiction, the setting is more than a backdrop; it is a character, a living entity that shapes the narrative, influences the characters, and transports readers across time. The authenticity of the setting is crucial to the success of the story, and this authenticity is born from meticulous research, an art in itself that brings the past to life, rekindles forgotten landscapes, and allows readers to walk hand-in-hand with the ghosts of history.

Researching locations and settings for historical fiction is a journey of discovery, a quest for the hidden gems of the past, the landscapes that once echoed with the footsteps of generations long gone. It is an endeavor that demands dedication, curiosity, and a deep respect for historical accuracy. As writers embark on this journey, they must keep in mind several key principles that enrich the authenticity and vividness of the setting.

As writers, our task is to become archaeologists of the past, sifting through these primary sources to uncover the details that paint a vivid picture of the setting. Whether it's exploring archives, reading old newspapers, or examining historical maps, the diligent pursuit of primary sources is the foundation upon which an authentic historical setting is built.

To truly understand a location, a writer must walk its terrain. Visiting historical sites, exploring the streets of old towns, and feeling the earth beneath one's feet can provide invaluable insights. The physical sensations, the sights, and the sounds of a place contribute to the depth of the setting, allowing writers to capture its essence with greater accuracy.

If your historical fiction is set in a medieval European town, visiting preserved medieval towns or the ruins of castles can be a transformative experience. The tactile and sensory details you gather during these visits will breathe life into your setting, making it tangible and real for your readers.

The historical setting is not a static entity; it is shaped by the context of its time. Understanding the historical context—social, political, economic, and cultural—enables writers to depict the setting in a way that aligns with the era in which the story unfolds.

For instance, researching a Victorian-era London street requires knowledge of the class divisions, the societal norms, and the prevailing architecture of that period. By integrating the context into your description, you create a more authentic and immersive experience for your readers, enabling them to travel back in time, to breathe the air of that era.

In this digital age, we have the privilege of virtual time travel. Online resources, digital archives, historical databases, and virtual tours of historical sites allow writers to access a wealth of information from the comfort of their homes. The Internet has become a treasure trove of historical knowledge, a portal that spans time and space.

Immersing oneself in these online resources not only provides valuable data but also offers inspiration and a sense of connection to the past. Virtual time travel supplements on-the-ground research, allowing writers to access a vast array of materials that might otherwise be out of reach.

Researching locations and settings for historical fiction requires a multidisciplinary approach. Writers must draw from various fields, including history, archaeology, geography, and even art. The more diverse the sources of information, the richer the tapestry of the setting.

For instance, if you're writing about an ancient Egyptian temple, studying the archaeological findings, examining the artwork and hieroglyphics, and understanding the religious practices of that period contribute to a comprehensive and vibrant portrayal. A multidisciplinary approach enables writers to capture not only the physical aspects of the setting but also its cultural and symbolic significance. If you have access to museums, such as the Met in New York or the British Museum in London, take advantage of the rich offerings of Egyptian artefacts on display there.

The quest for historical accuracy often benefits from the wisdom of experts. Consulting historians, archaeologists, and scholars can provide invaluable insights and clarifications, ensuring that the depiction of the setting aligns with historical truth.

If your historical fiction involves a specialized field or a particular era, seeking guidance from experts in that field can prevent inaccuracies and add depth to your portrayal. Expert advice can illuminate the nuances, answer questions, and provide a level of authenticity that enhances the reader's experience.

While research is essential for historical accuracy, it's important to strike a balance between facts and creativity. Historical fiction allows for imaginative exploration within the boundaries of the known past. The research provides a solid foundation, but creative liberties are often taken to fill in the gaps and bring the story to life.

Writers should view historical research as a springboard, a source of inspiration that guides their storytelling. The goal is not to replicate every detail but to create a setting that feels real and authentic. By blending factual accuracy with creative storytelling, writers can immerse readers in the past while weaving a compelling narrative.

The art of researching locations and settings for historical fiction is a dance between the past and the present. It is a journey of discovery that unearths forgotten landscapes, rekindles the flame of history, and weaves the threads of authenticity into the fabric of the story. As writers, our responsibility is to be stewards of the past, to honor its nuances, and to create settings that resonate with readers as vivid and timeless as the echoes of history itself.

Chapter 18

Recreating Historical Environments

In the enchanting realm of historical fiction, a writer's pen becomes a time machine, a conduit that transports readers to eras long past. The pages of these novels are imbued with the spirit of bygone days, and at the heart of this transformation lies the art of recreating historical environments. As readers, we find ourselves immersed in the grand tapestry of history, experiencing the sights, sounds, and emotions of another time. This is the magic, the allure, and the importance of recreating historical environments in the realm of storytelling.

Setting is more than just a backdrop; it is a living, breathing character in its own right. It has the power to shape the narrative, influence characters, and evoke emotions. Historical fiction, by its very nature, relies on the vivid depiction of the past, and the environment plays a pivotal role in this endeavor. The details of a historical setting—whether it's the cobbled streets of a medieval town, the opulence of a Renaissance palace, or the stark landscape of a wartime battleground—transport us to a different world.

The importance of historical environment goes beyond mere aesthetics. It serves as a bridge, a connection between the present and the past. Through the artful recreation of these environments, writers allow readers to step back in time, to breathe the air of a different era, and to gain a deeper understanding of the historical context that shaped the characters and events.

One of the key elements that sets historical fiction apart is its commitment to authenticity. The writer's ability to recreate historical environments with accuracy and attention to detail is what creates a sense of immersion for the reader. When the description of a 19th-century parlour transports us so vividly that we can practically smell the faint hint of lavender, or when the bustling streets of ancient Rome come alive with the sounds of hawkers and the echo of footsteps, we are drawn into the story with an almost palpable sense of reality.

Authenticity is not limited to physical details; it extends to the social norms, customs, and values of the era. It's in the way characters interact, the beliefs they hold, and the challenges they face. By weaving these elements into the historical environment, writers create a rich and compelling backdrop that resonates with readers on a deep and meaningful level.

Historical fiction serves as a time capsule, preserving the essence of the past for future generations. Through the recreation of historical environments, writers offer readers a unique opportunity to witness history firsthand. It's like peering through a window into a different time, gaining insight into the lives of people who lived, loved, and struggled in eras long gone.

Imagine the chance to stroll through the gardens of a Tudor-era castle, to witness the fervor of a suffragette rally, or to experience the turmoil of a Civil War battlefield. Through the pages of historical fiction, we can do just that. The careful attention to historical environments allows us to not only learn about history but to feel it, to experience the triumphs and tribulations of those who walked the same paths centuries before. Visit historial re-enactments to immerse yourself in the setting before writing... if you can.

Recreating historical environments is not just about escapism; it's also a powerful tool for understanding the human experience across time. As we immerse ourselves in these settings, we gain insights into the challenges and opportunities, the joys and hardships faced by people in different historical periods. We begin to see the threads that connect us to our ancestors, the common threads of humanity that transcend the ages.

Historical fiction has the power to inspire and to provoke reflection. As we delve into the recreated historical environments, we may find ourselves inspired by the resilience of characters who faced insurmountable odds, or by the courage of those who stood up for what they believed in. We may see parallels between the challenges of the past and the issues we face today, prompting us to reflect on the progress we've made or the work that still lies ahead.

These stories serve as a mirror, allowing us to examine our own beliefs, values, and actions in the context of the larger human story. The struggles, triumphs, and moral dilemmas faced by historical characters often prompt us to ask important questions about our own lives and the legacy we wish to leave behind. It allows us to step into the shoes of individuals from different cultures, backgrounds, and time periods. We begin to see the world through their eyes, to understand the challenges they faced, and to appreciate the similarities and differences that make us all human.

This gift of empathy is particularly important in today's world, where understanding and compassion are needed more than ever. Historical fiction reminds us that beneath the surface of time, we are all connected, all part of a larger narrative that spans centuries. By immersing ourselves in these environments, we cultivate empathy, and in doing so, we expand our capacity to understand, relate to, and connect with others, both past and present.

The importance of recreating historical environments in writing historical fiction lies in its lasting impact. These stories have the ability to educate, to entertain, and to inspire. They ignite a curiosity about the past, encouraging us to explore further, to seek out the true stories that inspired the fictional narratives.

Perhaps most importantly, historical fiction has the power to kindle a love for history itself. It ignites a passion for learning, a desire to uncover the hidden treasures of the past, and a recognition of the beauty and complexity of human history. And in the hands of skilled writers who master the art of recreating historical environments, this impact ripples outward, touching the lives of countless readers and leaving them forever changed.

As readers, we are fortunate to have writers who dedicate themselves to this art, who meticulously research, who craft their narratives with care, and who transport us to worlds long past. These storytellers carry the torch of history, illuminating the shadows of the past and ensuring that the stories of those who came before are not forgotten.

So, as we pick up a work of historical fiction, let us do so with gratitude for the writers who recreate historical environments, for the magic they weave, and for the timeless gift of being able to walk in the footsteps of history. Through these stories, we become time travelers, exploring the past with eager hearts, learning from the lessons it holds, and carrying its wisdom into the future.

Chapter 19
How Studying F. Scott Fitzgerald's Work Can Teach Us About Historical Research Techniques

Ah, the dance of ages! How marvelous it is to waltz with history, to grasp the faded threads of yesteryears and weave them into the tapestry of fiction. To don the cloak of a time traveler, not in flesh, but in the mind, to breathe life into moments long past, to resurrect characters who once walked these hallowed streets. This is the alchemy of historical fiction, a symphony played upon the strings of the past. And oh, what a beguiling melody it is.

In the realm of historical fiction, where the boundaries of time blur and the past beckons, the diligent hand of the researcher is a penultimate instrument. Like an explorer charting new lands, the historical fiction writer must traverse the annals of time, deciphering the clues, gathering the fragments of a bygone era, and then, with the artistry of a master craftsman, reimagine those distant days. The secret, dear reader, lies in the meticulous dance of historical research techniques.

The Quest for Authenticity

Before we embark upon this endeavor, let us pay our respects to authenticity. It is the North Star by which we navigate the waters of historical fiction. It cannot be overstated, but authenticity is more than a mere whisper of accuracy; it is the soul of the tale. It's the scratch of a gramophone that transports us to a different age, the aroma of a Prohibition-era speakeasy that tingles the senses, the clink of flapper pearls that resonate in our ears.

To achieve such authenticity, one must become an ardent scholar of the times. Dive into the dusty archives, where the sepia-stained pages hold secrets and stories waiting to be told. Bathe in the prose of the era, let the words of long-dead authors infuse your soul. Study the fashion, the etiquette, the peculiarities of the day; these are the brushstrokes that paint the canvas of your narrative.

Character: The Heartbeat of the Past

In the heart of historical fiction beats the pulse of its characters, and they, my dear friends, must be true to their time. A flapper with the mind of a Silicon Valley entrepreneur? Unthinkable! A knight from the Middle Ages pondering the mysteries of quantum physics? Absurd! Characters must embody the beliefs, aspirations, and limitations of the era. They are the product of their time, shaped by the events and ideologies swirling around them.

The historical researcher must become a psychologist of the past. Understand the societal norms, the class structures, the prevailing philosophies. Empathize with the struggles and triumphs of the people who walked those cobblestone streets or sailed those uncharted seas. It's not just about knowing the facts; it's about feeling the heartbeat of the past and channeling it through your characters.

Setting: The Canvas of Time

A story's setting is not merely a backdrop; it is a character in its own right. Whether it's the smoky jazz clubs of the Roaring Twenties or the fog-drenched streets of Victorian London, the setting must be as alive and vivid as the characters that inhabit it. Here, historical research is a painter's palette, each hue a brushstroke that brings the past to life.

Study the architecture, the geography, the climate, for they shape the atmosphere. But don't stop there; delve into the intangibles. What was the mood of the era? Was it a time of exuberant optimism or smoldering disillusionment? What were the whispers on the streets, the murmurs in the salons? Infuse these nuances into your setting, let them seep into the bones of your narrative.

The Art of Dialogue

Ah, the conversations of old! The way they spoke, the cadence of their words, the idioms that rolled off their tongues like pearls from a broken necklace. Mastering the art of historical dialogue is akin to learning a new language, one that allows you to converse with the past.

Research the slang, the expressions, the politeness codes of the era. Listen to the voices captured in ancient recordings, read the letters and diaries of the time. Let the language flow naturally, but with the subtle infusion of historical authenticity. A well-crafted dialogue not only advances the plot but also immerses the reader in the era, making them feel as if they're eavesdropping on a conversation through the corridors of time.

The Tapestry of History

As we thread together these techniques, a magnificent tapestry unfolds before us. Historical research is the loom upon which this tapestry is woven, and we, the storytellers, are the weavers. But, dear reader, do not be content with merely recounting facts. Weave the emotions, the dreams, the heartaches of those who lived before us. Make history breathe, make it alive.

F. Scott Fitzgerald himself once said, "You don't write because you want to say something; you write because you have something to say." Let your historical research be the catalyst for the stories you have to tell. Let it be the muse that whispers forgotten tales into your ears.

In this dance with history, we tread the delicate line between fact and fiction. We honor the past by preserving its essence, by giving voice to the forgotten, by breathing life into the archives. Let our words be the bridge that connects generations, the vessel that carries the stories of old into the hearts of the present.

So, dear writer, as you embark on your own journey through time, armed with the techniques of historical research, remember this: You are not just a writer; you are a sculptor of stories, a weaver of the echoes of time. And in your words, pens against the paper, *borne back ceaselessly into the past,* vibrant and immortal, an eternal testament to the power of historical fiction.

Chapter 20
Effective Research Methods and Resources

The Power of Primary Sources

Ah, the treasures of the past! Primary sources are the crown jewels of historical research, and in the hands of a skilled writer, they become the alchemical ingredients for crafting authentic historical fiction. These sources are the firsthand accounts, the original documents, the artifacts, and the diaries that hold the whispers of those who once lived.

Dive into archives and libraries, where fragile pages, yellowed with age, hold the secrets of history. Read personal letters, memoirs, and journals of individuals from the era you're exploring. The intimacy of these documents unveils the emotions, the language, and the daily struggles of the people, offering invaluable insights into their lives.

Visit museums and examine artifacts. The tactile connection to history, the feel of a quill pen or the weight of a dress, can spark inspiration and authenticity in your writing. Walk through historical sites, touch the walls that witnessed the past, listen to the echoes of generations gone by.

The World Wide Web: A Treasure Trove of Information

In our digital age, the internet is a treasure trove of historical information. However, like a vast library, it requires a discerning eye to separate the wheat from the chaff. Utilize reputable websites, academic databases, and online libraries. Look for sources from reputable institutions, such as universities, museums, and government archives.

Wikipedia can serve as a starting point for general information, but it should never be the sole source for historical research. Cross-reference information from multiple reputable sources to ensure accuracy. Explore online forums and discussion boards where historians and enthusiasts share knowledge and insights.

Books: The Cornerstones of Knowledge

Ah, the smell of aged paper, the weight of knowledge in one's hands. Books remain the cornerstone of research, especially in historical fiction. Seek out well-researched, scholarly works on the specific time period you're writing about. Look for books written by historians and experts in the field.

Fiction written during or shortly after the era you're exploring can be a goldmine of cultural and social insights. Authors like Dickens, Austen, or Twain provide a window into the world of their times. Don't neglect historical non-fiction either; books on social history, fashion, politics, and everyday life can offer a rich backdrop for your narrative.

Interact with Experts

The beauty of the human network is that it holds an array of expertise waiting to be tapped. Seek out historians, academics, and enthusiasts who specialize in the era you're writing about. Attend historical seminars, workshops, and conferences. Engage in conversations with experts, and don't be afraid to ask questions.

Local historical societies can be hidden gems. They often hold archives, organize talks, and provide resources that might not be easily accessible elsewhere. Museum curators and librarians can also offer guidance on locating rare materials or point you toward lesser-known sources.

Visual and Audio Resources

A picture is worth a thousand words, they say, and in historical fiction, this rings especially true. Visual resources such as photographs, paintings, and period advertisements can enrich your understanding of the era's aesthetics, fashion, and daily life. Explore the collections of museums and libraries, many of which have digital archives.

Audio recordings, music, and speeches from the time period can transport you to the atmosphere of the era. The cadence of speech, the tunes that echoed through the streets, the speeches that stirred hearts – these elements can be woven into the fabric of your narrative, immersing readers in the past.

Travel and Immersion

While not always feasible for every project, if you have the opportunity, traveling to locations that feature in your historical fiction can be immensely rewarding. The sights, sounds, and scents of the actual places can provide a visceral connection to the setting. Observe the architecture, walk the streets, and absorb the ambiance.

Immerse yourself in the culture and lifestyle of the era. Attend reenactments, festivals, and events that celebrate the past. Talk to locals, taste the food, and try to experience life as your characters would have.

Cultivate an Inquisitive Mind

The most effective research method, regardless of the

resources you use, is to cultivate an inquisitive mind. Approach your research with curiosity, and don't be afraid to follow tangents and explore unexpected topics. The connections you make during your research journey can often lead to the most intriguing and authentic elements in your historical fiction.

Effective research methods and resources are the threads that weave the past into the present. The alchemy of primary sources, the vast knowledge of books, the interconnectedness of the digital age, and the wisdom of experts combine to create a vivid tableau that captivates readers. Through visual and audio resources, the immersion of travel, and the spark of an inquisitive mind, historical fiction transforms from mere words on a page into a portal to another time.

As writers, we stand at the intersection of eras, holding the lantern of history to illuminate the path for our readers. We are the custodians of the past, tasked with breathing life into the forgotten, with giving voice to the echoes of time. Armed with effective research methods and the richness of resources, we embark on a quest to unveil the veil of time, to bring history to life, and to craft stories that resonate across the ages.

Chapter 21
Analyzing Primary and Secondary Sources

To weave a tale that transports readers to another time, a writer must be adept at deciphering the secrets held within primary and secondary sources. These sources, like windows to the past, offer invaluable insights that can breathe life into characters, settings, and narratives. In this essay, we'll delve into the intricacies of analyzing primary and secondary sources in the context of historical fiction, exploring the methods by which writers can unlock the treasure troves of the past to create compelling and authentic stories.

The Essence of Primary Sources

Primary sources are the raw materials of history. They are the artifacts, documents, records, and eyewitness accounts created by individuals who lived during the period being studied. These sources are the closest we can get to a direct connection with the past, and they hold the power to reveal the thoughts, emotions, and experiences of those who came before us.

For the historical fiction writer, primary sources are goldmines of authenticity. They provide the texture, the details, and the nuances that can make a story resonate with historical accuracy. To effectively analyze primary sources, one must approach them with a critical yet empathetic eye.

Understanding the Context

Context is the key that unlocks the meaning of primarysources. To truly grasp the significance of a source, the writer must situate it within the historical, social, and cultural context of the time period. What were the prevailing beliefs? What were the societal norms? What major events or conflicts were shaping the world at that moment?

For example, if you're examining a letter written by a soldier during World War I, consider the larger context of the war, the political climate, and the impact of the conflict on the lives of ordinary individuals. Understanding the context allows you to extract deeper meaning from the source and apply it effectively in your historical fiction.

Assessing Reliability

Reliability is a crucial aspect of primary source analysis. Not all sources are created equal; some may be biased, while others might be more objective. A careful evaluation of the source's credibility is essential.

Consider the authorship of the source. Was the author a direct witness to the events described, or is the account based on hearsay or secondhand information? Evaluate the author's background, motivations, and potential biases. Keep in mind that people from different social or political backgrounds may have varying perspectives on the same events.

For example, if you're analyzing a diary entry from a plantation owner during the 19th century, be aware of the potential biases related to issues of race, slavery, and socioeconomic status. Understand the author's position within the society of the time and how it might influence their views.

Uncovering Unspoken Messages

Sometimes, the most powerful messages in primary sources are the unspoken ones. Writers must read between the lines, deciphering the hidden meanings, emotions, and subtext within the source. It's the subtext that can often provide the richest material for historical fiction, allowing you to capture the underlying tensions, hopes, and fears of the era.

For instance, if you're analyzing a public speech delivered during the suffragette movement, pay attention to the language used, the metaphors employed, and the emotional tone. What is the speaker trying to convey beyond the literal words? What does the rhetoric reveal about the aspirations of the suffragettes and the societal resistance they faced? By uncovering these unspoken messages, you can infuse your historical fiction with layers of depth and authenticity.

The Role of Secondary Sources

While primary sources are the heartbeats of history, secondary sources play a vital role in shaping our understanding of the past. Secondary sources are interpretations, analyses, or summaries of primary sources created by historians, scholars, and experts. They provide a broader perspective, offering context, insights, and different viewpoints on historical events and periods.

For the historical fiction writer, secondary sources serve as guideposts, illuminating the landscape of the past and helping to navigate the complexities of historical accuracy. When analyzing secondary sources, writers must be mindful of their value, limitations, and potential biases.

Evaluating Expertise

One of the first steps in assessing a secondary source is to evaluate the expertise and credibility of the author. Consider the qualifications, background, and reputation of the historian or scholar who wrote the source. Have they published extensively in the field? Are they recognized as experts by their peers? A well-respected and knowledgeable author lends credibility to the secondary source.

For example, if you're researching the Victorian era for your historical fiction, look for works written by reputable historians who specialize in that period. Their expertise ensures that the information and analysis provided in the source are reliable.

Understanding Interpretation

Secondary sources are interpretations of primary sources, and as such, they reflect the author's perspective and interpretation of historical events. Writers must be aware of the potential biases or viewpoints that may influence the analysis presented in the secondary source.

Consider the author's theoretical framework, ideological stance, or any personal or scholarly biases that may impact their interpretation. Are they providing a balanced view, or does the source exhibit a particular slant? Understanding the interpretative lens through which the secondary source was crafted allows you to glean valuable insights while remaining aware of any potential biases.

For instance, if you're researching a biography of a historical figure for your fiction, be mindful of the author's perspective. Are they celebrating the figure as a hero, or are they critical of their actions? Recognizing the author's interpretation helps you extract useful information while considering different angles for your own narrative.

Contextualizing the Narrative

Secondary sources often offer a broader historical context that can enrich your understanding of the time period you're exploring in your historical fiction. They provide background information, thematic analysis, and connections to larger historical trends.

When analyzing a secondary source, consider how it fits into the larger historical narrative. Does it provide insights into the socio-political climate of the era? Does it offer a new perspective on well-known events? Understanding the contextual role of the secondary source allows you to integrate it effectively into your historical fiction, providing depth and a comprehensive understanding of the historical backdrop.

For example, if you're reading a scholarly article about the economic challenges faced by immigrants during the Industrial Revolution, consider how this information can inform the experiences of immigrant characters in your historical fiction. The broader context provided by the secondary source enriches the authenticity of your narrative.

In the world of historical fiction, the writer's ability to analyze primary and secondary sources is the key to unlocking the magic of the past. Primary sources offer the intimate details, the emotions, and the unspoken messages that infuse authenticity into characters and settings. Secondary sources provide the broader context, the expert interpretations, and the thematic analysis that enrich the historical narrative.

By understanding the context, assessing reliability, uncovering unspoken messages in primary sources, and evaluating expertise, interpretation, and contextual relevance in secondary sources, the historical fiction writer can craft a story that resonates with historical accuracy, transporting readers to another time while capturing the essence of the past. Through this skillful analysis, the writer becomes a time traveler, weaving the threads of history into a tapestry of unforgettable fiction.

Chapter 22
Avoiding Common Pitfalls in
Writing Historical Fiction

The allure of historical fiction lies in its ability to transport readers to another time, to evoke the sights, sounds, and emotions of a bygone era. However, the path to creating compelling historical fiction is fraught with challenges, particularly in the realm of research. Historical accuracy is the cornerstone of a successful historical fiction piece, but pitfalls await the unwary writer. Authors must navigate the treacherous waters of historical research, shedding light on common pitfalls and offering strategies to avoid them, ensuring that your historical fiction shines with authenticity and captivates the imagination of your readers.

The Siren Song of Anachronism

Anachronism is the bane of historical fiction, a siren song that lures writers into treacherous waters. Beware, for the anachronistic slip can shatter the illusion of historical authenticity. Anachronisms occur when elements from one era are mistakenly introduced into another, creating jarring inconsistencies that undermine the immersive experience.

To avoid this pitfall, meticulously research every detail, no matter how small. From clothing and language to technology and societal norms, ensure that every aspect of your narrative aligns with the time period you're portraying. Create a historical timeline and cross-reference details to prevent anachronisms. Keep a keen eye on idiomatic expressions, modern concepts, and anachronistic inventions that might unknowingly creep into your story.

The Mirage of Modern Values

Oh, the allure of modern sensibilities! It's tempting to infuse historical characters with contemporary attitudes and beliefs, but this path leads to a mirage. Historical characters must remain true to their era, adhering to the values, biases, and cultural norms of their time, even if those beliefs differ from our own.

To avoid this pitfall, immerse yourself in the mindset of the era you're portraying. Understand the prevailing societal norms, religious beliefs, and moral codes. Study the language, literature, and philosophies of the time. When creating characters, consider their background, education, and experiences within the context of their era. Allow your characters to evolve within the confines of historical authenticity, rather than imposing modern viewpoints on them.

The Labyrinth of Inaccurate Sources

Ah, the tantalizing allure of a juicy tidbit from an unreliable source! It's easy to fall into the trap of using inaccurate or biased materials in your research, leading your historical fiction astray. Not all sources are created equal, and writers must be vigilant in their selection and evaluation of research materials.

To avoid this pitfall, prioritize reputable and well-documented sources. Rely on primary sources whenever possible, but exercise caution in interpreting them. Cross-reference information from multiple reliable sources to ensure accuracy. Be wary of secondary sources that lack scholarly credibility or show signs of bias. Fact-check every piece of information before incorporating it into your historical fiction, and never sacrifice accuracy for the sake of a good story.

The Oubliette of Familiarity

Oh, the comfort of the familiar! It's easy to cling to the aspects of history that resonate with our existing knowledge, but this can create a narrow and one-dimensional portrayal of the past. Historical fiction must transcend our preconceived notions and explore the complexities of the era being depicted.

To avoid this pitfall, embrace the unfamiliar. Challenge your assumptions, question your biases, and seek out the lesser-known aspects of the time period. Delve into the details of daily life, explore the nuances of social hierarchy, and uncover the underrepresented voices of history. Let go of modern preconceptions and be open to discovering the intricate layers of the past that might not align with your initial expectations.

The Ignus Fatuss of Monoculturalism

History is a tapestry woven with threads of diversity, yet it's easy to fall into the pitfall of monoculturalism, creating a homogeneous portrayal of characters, settings, and experiences. The past was a mosaic of different cultures, ethnicities, and backgrounds, and ignoring this diversity flattens the richness of historical fiction.

To avoid this pitfall, celebrate diversity. Explore the multicultural facets of the era you're portraying. Incorporate characters from different backgrounds, religions, and walks of life. Showcase the interactions and tensions that arise from this diversity, and give voice to the marginalized and underrepresented communities of the time. Diversity not only adds depth to your historical fiction but also honors the full spectrum of human experiences throughout history.

The Quicksand of Excessive Detail

Ah, the allure of intricate detail! It's easy to become lost in the quicksand of excessive historical detail, drowning your narrative in minutiae that distract from the heart of the story. While historical accuracy is essential, inundating your readers with a barrage of details can overwhelm and detract from the emotional resonance of your fiction.

To avoid this pitfall, strike a balance between authenticity and storytelling. Choose details that enhance the atmosphere, setting, or character development, rather than inundating readers with information. Integrate historical details seamlessly into the narrative, using them to enrich the reader's experience rather than overshadowing the plot. Remember that less can often be more, allowing the emotional journey of your characters to shine through the historical backdrop.

The path to creating remarkable historical fiction is strewn with pitfalls, but armed with awareness and diligence, writers can navigate these challenges to craft stories that transport readers to another time while maintaining the integrity of historical accuracy. By avoiding anachronisms, refraining from imposing modern values on historical characters, using reliable sources, embracing the unfamiliar, celebrating diversity, and striking a balance between detail and storytelling, you can create a work of historical fiction that resonates with authenticity, captivates the imagination, and pays homage to the richness of the past. As you embark on your journey through the realms of history, remember that every step taken with care and integrity brings you closer to the treasure troves of historical authenticity.

Chapter 23
Incorporating Real Events into Your Plot

In the shadowed corners of forgotten libraries, where dust-laden tomes recount the tales of bygone eras, there exists a whispered pact between history and the creative spirit. It is within the pages of time-worn manuscripts that the writer of historical fiction discovers the magic of incorporating actual events into the plot. Ah, what a wondrous dance it is, as the ink of history mingles with the quill of imagination, and the result is a tapestry that captures the essence of a moment, the heartbeat of a generation. As I endeavor to elucidate the art of this delicate weaving, permit me, dear reader, to don the mantle of Victor Hugo, and together, we shall explore the symphony of history within the realm of fiction.

The foundations of authenticity are built upon the bedrock of actual events. These events serve as the scaffolding upon which characters ascend, the landscapes they traverse, and the conflicts they confront. To ignore history is to forfeit the essence of the past, to render one's fiction adrift in the sea of contrivance.

Imagine, if you will, a tale set amidst the tumultuous days of the French Revolution. The Revolution itself is a tempestuous canvas, painted with fervent ideals, thunderous guillotines, and whispers of liberation. To weave a narrative in this era without invoking the stormy tides of revolution, without the echo of the National Assembly or the despair of the Bastille, would be a disservice to the very soul of the story.

Or consider, for a moment, the Battle of Waterloo. In the hands of a skilled historical fiction writer, this legendary clash between Napoleon and Wellington becomes more than a chronicle of troop movements; it becomes a canvas upon which characters, both real and imaginary, navigate the currents of fate. Picture a young officer, his heart pounding amidst the thunderous cannonade, his destiny intertwined with the tumultuous outcome of the battle. His story, a thread in the grand narrative of Waterloo, allows readers to witness the human face of history, to grasp the impact of that momentous day on the lives of individuals.

Within the confines of actual events, the historical fiction writer discovers a paradox of freedom. It is within the boundaries of historical accuracy that the imagination truly soars. These events, like a symphony's notes on a stave, provide a structure, a rhythm, but within this framework, the creative spirit finds liberty.

Imagine, if you dare, a tale set in the ancient city of Pompeii, on the eve of that fateful eruption. The eruption, a factual cataclysm, becomes the backdrop against which a forbidden love unfolds, a dramatic interplay of human emotions against the canvas of impending doom. Here, the historical event serves as both the stage and the catalyst, allowing the writer to explore the depths of human passion within the shadow of impending tragedy.

The incorporation of actual events into the plot is a delicate dance, a waltz between the real and the imagined. Characters, whether drawn from the annals of history or conjured from the depths of one's creative wellspring, must navigate this intricate choreography. The interactions between these characters, both real and imagined, must ring true, honoring the historical context while breathing life into the narrative.

Another example: Picture a renowned philosopher exchanging ideas with a young, aspiring thinker, their dialogues echoing within the chambers of history. The fictional character, a vessel through which the reader experiences these discussions, becomes the conduit between the known and the unknown, the bridge that allows the writer to delve into the intellectual currents of the era.

Imagine a tale set during the Renaissance, a period of rebirth and enlightenment. Within this narrative, the reader witnesses the intellectual fervor of the era, the clash of ideas between humanism and tradition, the artistic awakening that reshaped the world. Through the eyes of characters, both historical and fictional, the reader becomes a participant in the vibrant tapestry of the Renaissance, feeling the pulse of progress and the tension of transformation.

Consider a narrative set in the midst of the American Civil War. The conflict, a monumental event in the shaping of a nation, becomes the crucible in which characters are forged. A young nurse tends to wounded soldiers, a Confederate officer grapples with the moral dilemmas of war, and a former slave dreams of emancipation. These characters, their stories woven into the fabric of the Civil War, exemplify the intimate connection between the individual and the grand sweep of history.

By weaving these events into the narrative, the historical fiction writer ensures that the whispers of history are not lost to the winds of time.

Imagine, if you will, a tale set amidst the backdrop of the Great Fire of London. The flames, a historical cataclysm, become the crucible in which characters face adversity, discover resilience, and forge new beginnings. The story of a humble bookseller, his shop consumed by the inferno, becomes a metaphor for the resilience of the human spirit in the face of destruction. Through this narrative, the reader bears witness to the transformative power of history, the way it shapes individuals and communities alike.

As I pen these words, I am reminded of the power of history's embrace. It is a dance, a symphony, a tapestry, and within its folds, the past finds a voice. The events that shaped our world, the struggles, triumphs, and tragedies of those who came before, are not mere footnotes in the pages of time; they are the very heartbeats of our collective narrative.

Infusing actual events into the plot of historical fiction is more than a technique; it is a responsibility. It is the duty of the writer to honor the legacy of the past, to bear witness to the stories that shaped our world, and to ensure that the whispers of history continue to resonate through the corridors of time. As you embark on your own journey through the realm of historical fiction, may you, too, heed this whispered pact, weaving the threads of actual events into the tapestry of your narrative, and in doing so, perpetuating the eternal dialogue between history and the human spirit.

Chapter 24
Using Historical Events as Plot Anchors

In the magical realm of historical fiction, where the present merges with the past, where imagination weaves threads of authenticity, and where the echoes of bygone eras resonate in the hearts of readers, one essential technique stands as a guiding star: the use of historical events as plot anchors. Within the grand tapestry of historical fiction, these events serve as pivotal points, anchoring the narrative in the reality of the past while allowing the creative spirit to unfurl its wings. In this article, we shall embark on a journey through the art of employing historical events as plot anchors, exploring the power, challenges, and enchantment this technique brings to the realm of storytelling.

Plot anchors, as forged from the iron of historical events, provide the foundation upon which the narrative stands. They are the landmarks that guide the writer through the tumultuous waters of creativity, ensuring that the story remains rooted in the authenticity of the past. These anchors serve multiple crucial roles within the framework of historical fiction.

First and foremost, plot anchors lend historical fiction its unique flavor of verisimilitude. They connect the characters, the settings, and the conflicts to the real-world events that shaped the era in which the story is set. This connection is not a mere embellishment; it is the secret ingredient that infuses the narrative with the aroma of authenticity, allowing readers to immerse themselves in the time period, to taste the emotions, to experience the triumphs and tribulations of those who lived in that age.

Moreover, plot anchors provide a framework for the narrative's structure. They create a sense of continuity, linking the events of the story to the historical milestones that dot the landscape. These anchors serve as points of reference, allowing the writer to navigate the complex interplay of character development, conflict resolution, and thematic exploration within the broader context of historical events.

Finally, plot anchors amplify the emotional impact of the narrative. They give the characters stakes in the unfolding events, weaving their personal journeys into the fabric of history. When characters are anchored to actual historical events, their triumphs become intertwined with the triumphs of the era, their struggles resonate with the struggles of their contemporaries, and their resolutions echo the broader themes of the time. The emotional resonance of the narrative is heightened, as readers witness the individual's story within the larger context of historical significance.

The essence of using historical events as plot anchors lies in the delicate dance of blending fact and fiction. The writer must navigate this intricate choreography, seamlessly weaving the threads of imagination into the tapestry of historical reality. This fusion is not a collision of worlds but a harmonious symphony, where the notes of history and the melodies of creativity intertwine to create a narrative that is both authentic and enchanting.

The key to this harmonious blend is thorough research. The writer must delve into the annals of history, unearthing the details, the nuances, and the emotional currents of the chosen historical event. Immerse yourself in primary sources, study the accounts, letters, diaries, and records of the time. Listen to the voices of those who lived through the event, capturing the cadence of their language, the hopes, the fears, the dreams that filled their hearts. Understand the context, the societal norms, the cultural backdrop, for these are the brushstrokes that paint the backdrop against which your fictional tale unfolds.

Once armed with the treasure trove of historical knowledge, the writer must exercise the art of creative interpretation. This is where the magic happens, where the imagination breathes life into the historical event, infusing it with fictional characters, personal conflicts, and thematic exploration. This is not a mere retelling of history, but a reimagining, a layering of the fictional upon the factual.

Let us consider an example. Imagine a historical event such as the signing of the Declaration of Independence. This momentous event, a cornerstone of American history, becomes the plot anchor for a tale set during the American Revolution. The writer meticulously researches the details of the signing, the personalities of the signers, the political climate of the time. These factual elements serve as the scaffold upon which the writer builds a story of intrigue, personal sacrifices, and the clash of ideologies. The fictional characters, perhaps a young revolutionary torn between loyalty to family and loyalty to the cause, add depth and emotional resonance to the historical event. Their personal struggles become entwined with the broader struggle for independence, allowing readers to witness the intersection of the personal and the historical.

The art lies in knowing when to adhere to historical accuracy and when to exercise creative license. While the factual foundation must remain steadfast, the creative spirit must be free to explore the uncharted territories of imagination. Let the historical event guide the narrative's trajectory, but allow the characters to breathe, to surprise, to evolve within the bounds of historical authenticity.

Using historical events as plot anchors is a challenging

endeavor, but the rewards are bountiful. One of the primary challenges is striking the balance between historical accuracy and storytelling. The writer must resist the temptation to become a mere chronicler of history, recounting events without the vibrancy of fictional life. Conversely, the writer must also avoid the pitfall of sacrificing historical authenticity for the sake of a convenient plot twist.

To overcome this challenge, meticulous planning is essential. Outline the narrative, identifying the historical events that will anchor the plot. Determine how these events align with the character arcs, the conflicts, and the themes you wish to explore. Chart the emotional journey of your characters within the broader context of history. By understanding the interplay between the fictional and the factual, you can strike that delicate balance, allowing the plot anchors to enhance the narrative without overwhelming it.

Another challenge lies in avoiding the trap of predictability. The use of well-known historical events as plot anchors can sometimes lead to a sense of inevitability, where readers anticipate the outcome because they are familiar with the real-world event. This sense of predictability can diminish the tension and emotional impact of the narrative.

To overcome this challenge, consider incorporating lesser-known aspects of the historical event. Focus on the personal stories, the behind-the-scenes struggles, the untold perspectives that history might have overlooked. Delve into the human side of the event, revealing the emotions, the conflicts, the sacrifices that were part of the larger historical moment. By shedding light on the lesser-known aspects, you can create an element of surprise and intrigue, keeping readers engaged and invested in the narrative's outcome.

The rewards of using historical events as plot anchors are manifold. The resonance of the narrative is deepened, as readers connect with the characters on a personal level within the broader context of history. The authenticity of the setting and the emotional weight of the events add layers of depth to the storytelling, making the fictional journey a profound exploration of the human experience within the confines of historical reality.

Moreover, the use of historical plot anchors provides an opportunity to educate, to illuminate, and to inspire. Through your fictional tale, readers can gain a deeper understanding of the historical event, its significance, and its impact on the lives of individuals. This educational aspect of historical fiction enriches the reader's experience, fostering a sense of appreciation for the past and a curiosity to explore further.

Each historical event serves as a unique color, a distinct texture, contributing to the overall richness of the narrative. The characters, the conflicts, and the themes become the loom through which these threads are woven, creating a masterpiece that captures the essence of the past while igniting the spark of creativity.

As you embark on your journey through the realm of historical fiction, may you embrace the power of historical events as plot anchors. Let them guide your narrative, infusing it with authenticity, depth, and resonance. But in doing so, never forget the magic of the creative spirit, the ability to breathe life into the past, to reimagine history through the lens of fiction, and to offer readers a journey that transcends time and bridges the gap between imagination and reality. With historical events as your anchors, may your historical fiction become a vessel, carrying the whispers of history into the hearts of those who embark upon its pages, leaving them forever enriched by the tapestry you've woven.

Chapter 25
The Dance of Tension and Certainty

Where the past meets the imagination, where the echoes of bygone eras resonate with the present, a unique and delicate dance unfolds—one that involves creating tension even when the outcome is known. How can a writer captivate readers when historical events are etched in the annals of time? How can the narrative spark anticipation and intrigue when the destination is familiar? In this essay, we shall embark on a journey through the art of creating tension by using known outcomes in historical fiction, exploring the subtle alchemy that transforms certainty into a canvas for suspense and discovery.

At the heart of using known outcomes as a source of tension lies the power of historical anchors. These anchors are the events, the turning points, the milestones in the past that lend authenticity and context to the narrative. They are the touchstones that ground the story in historical reality, allowing readers to traverse the landscape of bygone eras. From legendary battles and political upheavals to significant discoveries and societal transformations, these historical anchors form the backdrop against which characters navigate their journeys.

The beauty of historical anchors is that they provide a sense of certainty, a foundation upon which the writer builds the narrative. Readers, often possessing a basic familiarity with the historical context, enter the story with an understanding of the broader events that shaped the era. The challenge, then, lies in taking this knowledge, this awareness of the known outcomes, and transforming it into a source of tension that propels the narrative forward.

One powerful way to create tension within the framework of known outcomes is through a character-centric approach. The characters, their desires, fears, and conflicts, become the fulcrum upon which tension pivots. As they navigate the currents of history, their personal journeys, dreams, and struggles take center stage, even as the larger historical events loom in the background.

Consider a historical fiction set during the American Civil War. The outcome of the war is a known fact—the Union prevails, the Confederacy falls. But within this historical certainty, the writer can craft characters with personal stakes, weaving their destinies into the broader context of the conflict. The tension arises not from the uncertainty of the war's outcome, but from the emotional arcs of the characters.

A young nurse, torn between loyalty to her family's Southern heritage and her belief in the Union's cause, grapples with the moral dilemmas of a divided nation. A wounded Confederate soldier, seeking redemption for his past actions, finds himself in an unexpected alliance with a Union officer. These characters, their choices, their interactions, become the conduits through which readers experience the emotional impact of the Civil War. The known outcome of the war serves as a canvas upon which their personal struggles are painted, intensifying the tension and investment in their stories.

The key to utilizing known outcomes as a source of tension is creating a sense of suspense that transcends the historical certainty. Suspense arises not from the question of "what will happen" but from the anticipation of "how it will happen." The writer must engage readers' curiosity, leading them on a path of discovery, even as they possess a basic understanding of the ultimate destination.

To achieve this, the writer can focus on the intricacies, the twists and turns within the historical events themselves. These are the moments that history books often gloss over, the lesser-known aspects, the behind-the-scenes struggles that add depth and intrigue. The writer can delve into the human stories within the broader historical narrative, shedding light on the untold perspectives, the uncharted territories of emotion and conflict.

Returning to our American Civil War example, imagine a subplot that delves into the covert operations of spies on both sides. The characters involved, their motivations, their alliances, create a web of suspense within the larger context of the war. The reader knows the war's outcome, but the journey through the world of espionage, the twists and betrayals, the risks and secrets, becomes a source of intrigue. The historical outcome serves as the anchor, but the suspense arises from the unpredictability of the characters' paths within that historical framework.

Another fascinating way to create tension using known outcomes is to explore alternative histories, branching off from the established events. This technique allows the writer to introduce elements of uncertainty, leading readers down a path where the historical outcome might not be as predetermined as they thought.

Consider a historical fiction set during the time of the French Revolution. The writer can introduce a twist where a key historical figure survives an assassination attempt, altering the course of the Revolution. The reader, familiar with the historical fact that the Revolution led to significant changes in France, is now confronted with the possibility of a different outcome. This alternative history becomes a fertile ground for tension, as characters and readers grapple with the uncertainty of what might have been, navigating a world where the historical anchors are slightly adrift.

In this scenario, the writer must tread carefully, balancing the introduction of alternative histories with the respect for the historical context. The goal is not to rewrite history but to explore the "what-ifs" within the boundaries of plausibility. By doing so, the writer can create a captivating sense of tension as characters navigate the uncharted waters of this altered historical landscape.

Known outcomes can also serve as platforms for exploring profound themes and moral dilemmas. By anchoring the narrative in historical events, the writer can delve into the complexities of human nature, ethics, and the consequences of choices.

Consider a historical fiction set during the aftermath of World War II. The historical outcome—the defeat of the Axis powers —is established. But within this context, the writer can craft a story that explores the aftermath of war, the challenges of rebuilding, the personal struggles of individuals coming to terms with their actions during the conflict.

A character, a former soldier haunted by his role in a wartime atrocity, must grapple with guilt, redemption, and the pursuit of a meaningful life in the post-war world. The known outcome of the war forms the backdrop for this exploration of morality and personal responsibility. The tension arises not from the war's outcome but from the emotional weight of the character's choices, from the quest for forgiveness, and the search for a path toward redemption.

In the intricate dance of historical fiction, the known outcomes serve as partners, guiding the steps of the narrative, but leaving room for the unpredictable twists of character, emotion, and exploration. Through a character-centric approach, a sense of suspense, alternative histories, and the exploration of themes and moral dilemmas, the writer transforms historical certainty into a canvas for tension and discovery.

As the writer navigates this delicate dance, the known outcomes become the foundation upon which the creative spirit can soar. The resonance of history is not diminished but enhanced, as readers engage with characters who live and breathe within the historical context, experiencing the emotional impact of their personal journeys. It is this interplay between historical anchors and the uncharted territories of fiction that gives rise to the magic of historical fiction, where the past comes alive, where the echoes of time harmonize with the melodies of imagination, and where the dance of tension and certainty continues to captivate and inspire.

Chapter 26
Dialogue in Historical Context

In the annals of literature, where the echoes of bygone eras softly linger, one truth remains as steadfast as a well-maintained bonnet ribbon: the exquisite importance of period dialogue in the art of crafting historical fiction. As I set forth on this literary journey to elucidate the nuances and charms of this essential component, permit me, dear reader, to draw upon the penmanship of the inimitable Jane Austen herself—a masterful wordsmith whose timeless works exemplify the grace and eloquence of period dialogue.

The Quintessential Quill of Authenticity

The fundamental principle that unfurls before us, like a country ballroom adorned with the finest silks and flowers, is the pursuit of authenticity. A writer of historical fiction must not merely capture the tapestry of an era's costumes, manners, and architecture; they must ensnare the very essence of the time, and what better conduit for such an endeavor than the spoken word?

Period dialogue, like an intricately choreographed quadrille, dances upon the page, creating a symphony of voices that transports readers to the heart of the past. It is the subtlest of brushstrokes that paints a vivid portrait of the era's lexicon, social mores, and the ebb and flow of conversations that once filled drawing rooms and countryside lanes. Without the delicate cadence of period dialogue, the historical fiction narrative, no matter how meticulously researched, risks becoming an empty shell—an elegantly gowned mannequin lacking the soul of genuine human interaction.

A Cultural Lens Through Time

The significance of period dialogue is akin to a magnifying glass through which we, as readers and writers, peer back into history's vibrant tapestry. Every era carries with it a unique linguistic and cultural fingerprint, a collection of phrases, expressions, and sensibilities that shape the way its inhabitants communicate. To dismiss this aspect would be akin to overlooking the vibrant hues of a Regency ballgown or the intricate architecture of a Gothic cathedral.

Consider, if you will, the genteel society of Austen's own time —the early 19th century. The polite exchanges, the subtle flirtations, the meticulous politeness interwoven with hidden meanings—all come alive through the period dialogue in her novels. From the decorous parlance of "Mr. Darcy" to the gentle reproach of "You must allow me to tell you how ardently I admire and love you" in the epistolary art of "Mr. Darcy" himself, Austen's characters are not mere inhabitants of the Regency period; they are its living embodiment, speaking in the dialect of their time, revealing the societal norms, expectations, and subtle complexities of their world.

In crafting historical fiction, period dialogue serves as the key to unlocking this cultural treasure chest. It transports readers to the heart of the era, allowing them to experience not only the grand events but also the everyday interactions, the intricacies of class distinctions, the subtleties of courtship, and the unspoken truths that define the human experience of that time.

The Dance of Language and Character

Ah, but it is not enough to merely sprinkle one's narrative with archaic phrases and quaint expressions, as if playing a parlour game of "Guess the Era." The true mastery of period dialogue lies in its seamless integration with the characters themselves—their personalities, backgrounds, aspirations, and motivations. It is here, in the exquisite dance between language and character, that period dialogue ascends to its highest form of artistry.

In the world of Austen's "Pride and Prejudice," each character possesses a distinct voice, a linguistic signature that reveals not only their societal standing but also the intricacies of their souls. The refined eloquence of Mr. Darcy stands in stark contrast to the effusive exuberance of Lydia Bennet. The sly wit of Elizabeth Bennet engages in delightful verbal duels with the dry humor of Mr. Bennet, while the artless naiveté of Mr. Collins echoes like an off-key piano note against the refined symphony of the Bingley sisters. It is through this interplay of language and character that Austen's canvas becomes alive with the diverse hues of human nature.

In historical fiction, period dialogue allows characters to speak not only to their contemporaries but also to the readers across the expanse of time. A well-crafted dialogue reveals the motivations, desires, and inner conflicts of characters while shedding light on the society they inhabit. The word choices, the sentence structures, the subtleties of language become windows through which we glimpse their world, their relationships, and their place within the tapestry of history.

The Bridge Between Eras

Beyond its intrinsic beauty and authenticity, period dialogue serves as a bridge, connecting the past with the present, creating a timeless resonance that transcends the boundaries of time. When readers engage with historical fiction, they seek not only to learn about the past but to feel it, to breathe the same air as those who lived in the era they explore. Period dialogue provides this bridge, allowing modern readers to enter the world of the past, to experience the emotions, aspirations, and challenges of characters as if they were their contemporaries.

The enduring appeal of Austen's works is a testament to this power of period dialogue as a bridge between eras. Her novels, set in the early 19th century, continue to capture the hearts of readers in the 21st century. Through her period dialogue, Austen invites us into the drawing rooms, the social gatherings, and the intimate conversations of her characters. We feel their hopes, their disappointments, their follies, and their growth as if they were our friends, our confidantes, our kindred spirits.

As writers of historical fiction, our duty is to construct a similar bridge, to create a narrative that resonates not only with the era it portrays but also with the hearts and minds of modern readers. Through period dialogue, we offer readers the opportunity to connect with the past, to understand the universality of human emotions, and to find relevance in the lives of characters separated by centuries.

The Symphony of Period Dialogue

Period dialogue is the thread that weaves authenticity, cultural exploration, character depth, and timeless resonance. It allows readers to step into the shoes of those who lived in the past, to converse with historical figures, and to immerse themselves in the society, the manners, and the language of bygone eras.

Like the finest composition by a maestro, period dialogue orchestrates a symphony of voices that harmonize with the era's setting, the characters' personalities, and the narrative's themes. It is the subtlety of language, the intonation of emotion, the expression of societal norms, and the unspoken truths that elevate historical fiction from mere storytelling to a transformative experience.

As writers, let us embrace the exquisite challenge of crafting period dialogue, for it is through this delicate art that we bring the past to life, that we offer readers a passport to another time, and that we honor the legacy of those who have gone before us. Let our words resonate with the cadence of history, let our characters speak in the dialect of their era, and let our narratives become a gateway through which readers can step into the whispered echoes of the past, experiencing the joys, the sorrows, and the profound humanity that transcends the confines of time.

Chapter 27
Capturing Authentic Language and Speech

To craft dialogue that resonates with the era, society, and characters of the past requires a keen understanding of linguistic nuances, social context, and the timeless essence of human communication. In this discourse, we shall embark on a journey to unravel the secrets of mastering authentic language and speech in historical fiction, a journey that echoes through the corridors of time and brings the past alive through the spoken word.

Dive into the Archives: Research with Precision

The cornerstone of crafting authentic language and speech lies in thorough research. Immerse yourself in the primary sources of the era you're portraying—letters, diaries, newspapers, literary works, and historical documents. These hidden treasures offer insights into the vocabulary, phrases, idioms, and sentence structures of the time. Study not only the formal language but also the colloquialisms, slang, and informal speech patterns that reveal the true texture of communication.

For example, if your historical fiction is set in Victorian England, read letters exchanged between individuals of various social classes. Note the distinctions in language between the upper echelons of society and the working class. Pay attention to the subtleties in address, formality, and expressions of emotion. This meticulous research will serve as your compass, guiding you through the linguistic landscape of the era.

The Art of Balance: Historical Accuracy and Accessibility

While historical accuracy is paramount, it's essential to strike a balance between authenticity and readability. Language evolves, and what might have been commonplace in the past could be perplexing to modern readers. The goal is not to bewilder but to transport, so weave period-appropriate language into the narrative without overwhelming readers with unfamiliar terms.

Incorporate historical terminology organically, using context to aid comprehension. If a term is integral to the scene or the character's personality, introduce it gradually and offer subtle explanations. When characters converse, intersperse period expressions with familiar language, allowing readers to navigate the dialogue effortlessly while still capturing the essence of the era.

The Social Dance: Reflecting Class, Culture, and Context

In historical fiction, dialogue is a window through which readers glimpse the societal norms, class distinctions, and cultural nuances of the era. Different social classes, regions, and cultural backgrounds shape language use, creating a rich tapestry of expression. Characters from diverse backgrounds should reflect these distinctions in their speech, lending authenticity to their interactions.

Imagine a story set in the Elizabethan era. Characters from the nobility would employ elaborate language, employing formal address and grandiloquent phrases. In contrast, characters from the lower classes might use simpler, more direct speech. Infuse dialogue with these distinctions, allowing the language to convey not only individual personalities but also the layers of society that shape their lives.

Reading Between the Lines: Unspoken Communication

In historical fiction, dialogue extends beyond the words spoken—it's a realm of unspoken communication, hidden meanings, and subtle gestures. The art of crafting authentic speech involves understanding the nonverbal cues that reveal character dynamics and the underlying currents of emotion.

Explore the language of body language, eye contact, and facial expressions as documented in historical accounts. In a tale set during the Renaissance, characters might convey deference through elaborate bows and curtseys, while a sideways glance might hold more significance than spoken words. By incorporating these nonverbal elements, you breathe life into the characters and immerse readers in the complex dance of human interaction.

The Voice of Individuality: Character-Centric Language

Each character possesses a distinct voice—a linguistic fingerprint that arises from their personality, background, and experiences. The language they use is a mirror reflecting their inner world. Mastering character-centric language is the pinnacle of authenticity in historical fiction, for it transcends the era and speaks to the universal essence of human nature.

Consider a character embroiled in the tumultuous events of the French Revolution. Their language might embody a mix of hope and fear, bravado and vulnerability, as they navigate the uncertainties of the time. Characters from different walks of life should showcase their uniqueness through dialogue. A well-read scholar might employ elaborate metaphors, while a street-smart trader might use succinct, pragmatic language.

The Quill of Suggestion: Implied Dialogues

An artful technique in historical fiction is the use of implied dialogues—interactions that occur without direct speech but are conveyed through context, actions, and reactions. These unspoken dialogues unveil emotions, relationships, and conflicts with subtlety, allowing readers to engage in a form of literary deciphering.

Picture a scene in a medieval castle where a servant enters a room and a noblewoman lowers her gaze. The implied dialogue reveals a hierarchy of power, social norms, and the unspoken understanding between the two characters. Implied dialogues infuse layers of depth into the narrative, inviting readers to become active participants in uncovering the meaning behind the words left unsaid.

Editing as a Polishing Loom: Refining and Elevating

The crafting of authentic language and speech doesn't end with the initial draft—it's a continuous refinement process. As you revise, polish the dialogue, ensuring it flows naturally and authentically. Read it aloud to gauge its rhythm and cadence, allowing your ears to guide your revisions. Trim excessive phrasing while preserving the character's unique voice, seeking that balance between authenticity and accessibility.

Remember that historical accuracy doesn't preclude elegance. Language, even in the past, was capable of beauty and eloquence. Seek out literary works from the era, absorbing their artistry and integrating it into your dialogue. The quill of suggestion and implication, when honed, can create conversations that sparkle with intrigue, wit, and layers of meaning.

In the Shadows of the Past: A Living Tapestry of Speech

To write historical fiction is to embark on a journey to the past—a journey that relies on the mastery of authentic language and speech to bring the echoes of bygone eras to life. As writers, we are both historians and artists, weaving a living tapestry of speech that transports readers through time.

Authentic language and speech are not mere ornaments but the essence of historical fiction, imbuing it with texture, resonance, and vitality. Through meticulous research, thoughtful balance, social and character nuances, implied dialogues, and careful editing, we can paint dialogue that is not only authentic but also a bridge connecting readers to the emotions, experiences, and heartbeats of those who lived in the past. In the eloquent echoes of their spoken words, we find the magic that breathes life into historical fiction, capturing the essence of human communication that transcends the boundaries of time.

Chapter 28
Handling Dialects and Vernacular

In the intricate tapestry of historical fiction, dialects and vernaculars are like vibrant threads, weaving authenticity, diversity, and depth into the narrative. The challenge, however, lies in handling these linguistic nuances with care and precision. When employed skillfully, dialects and vernaculars enrich the storytelling, immersing readers in the era and region portrayed. This exploration delves into the delicate art of incorporating dialects and vernaculars in historical fiction, a journey that requires a keen understanding of cultural context, readability, and the balance between authenticity and accessibility.

The Essence of Authenticity

Dialects and vernaculars are the linguistic embodiment of a specific time, place, and culture. They capture the rhythm of speech, the idioms, and the distinct flavor of a region or community. In historical fiction, these linguistic nuances serve as portals through which readers can step into the world of the past, allowing them to experience the era and its inhabitants more intimately.

To achieve authenticity, diligent research is essential. Study primary sources from the period and location you're portraying. Letters, diaries, local literature, and recordings, if available, provide invaluable insights into the language spoken at the time. Pay attention to phonetic differences, unique expressions, and grammatical idiosyncrasies that distinguish the dialect or vernacular.

Balancing Authenticity with Readability

While authenticity is paramount, it's equally crucial to strike a balance between historical accuracy and readability. Dialects and vernaculars, if used excessively or without consideration for the reader's comprehension, can hinder the flow of the narrative, leading to confusion and frustration.

Consider the audience for whom you're writing. If the chosen dialect or vernacular is unfamiliar to your readers, introduce it gradually, providing context and explanations where necessary. A reader should be able to immerse themselves in the dialogue without constant interruptions to decipher the meaning. The goal is to evoke the atmosphere and spirit of the era without creating an impenetrable linguistic barrier.

Character Consistency and Variation

Incorporating dialects and vernaculars becomes particularly meaningful when it's employed to distinguish characters from various backgrounds. Characters hailing from different regions, social classes, or cultural communities may speak in distinct ways. This not only reflects the diversity within the historical setting but also adds depth to the characters, showcasing their origins, upbringing, and interactions with the world around them.

For instance, imagine a historical fiction set during the American Civil War. Characters from the Southern states might speak with a Southern drawl, while those from the Northern states might have a different cadence. A character from a rural background might use colloquial expressions, while a character from an urban setting may employ more refined language. Consistency in character-specific dialects and vernaculars is crucial to maintaining authenticity.

Subtle Hints and Context Clues

A masterful technique in handling dialects and vernaculars is to provide subtle hints and context clues. Instead of explicitly transcribing every word in the dialect, sprinkle the narrative with hints that suggest the character's unique way of speaking. These hints can be in the form of syntax, word choices, or the occasional use of a regional expression.

For example, if a character speaks with a strong Scottish brogue, occasionally use Scottish colloquialisms or structure their sentences in a way that hints at their accent. The occasional "aye" or "wee" can add flavor without overwhelming the reader. The balance lies in offering enough hints to evoke the character's speech patterns while preserving the flow of the dialogue.

Dialogic Delicacies: Choosing the Right Words

When transcribing dialects or vernaculars, select words that capture the essence of the character's speech without devolving into caricature. Avoid stereotypes or offensive portrayals that could detract from the authenticity and respect of the character. The goal is to honor the character's unique voice while remaining sensitive to modern sensibilities.

Additionally, consider the readability of the dialogue. Certain dialects or vernaculars may be challenging to read, especially when presented extensively. Use moderation and ensure that the reader can follow the conversation without stumbling over the words. Strike a balance that captures the flavor of the dialect while preserving the narrative's flow.

Editing as a Polishing Quill

As with any element of writing, the art of incorporating dialects and vernaculars evolves during the editing process. Revisiting the dialogue allows you to refine and polish, ensuring that the authenticity of the language does not overshadow the readability and engagement of the narrative.

Read the dialogue aloud to gauge its rhythm and flow. Ensure that it feels natural and true to the character while keeping the reader's comprehension in mind. Trim excessive phonetic transcription while preserving the spirit of the dialect or vernacular. Seek feedback from beta readers or critique partners, especially those familiar with the era or linguistic nuances you're portraying.

Implied Culture: Beyond Language

Dialects and vernaculars extend beyond mere language—they hint at the culture, social norms, and worldview of the characters and the era they inhabit. Use these linguistic nuances to subtly reveal the character's background, values, and interactions with their environment.

Consider a historical fiction set in medieval Europe. A character from a fishing village may use nautical terms in their speech, reflecting their connection to the sea. Another character from a noble family might employ more formal language, emphasizing their education and social standing. These subtle details paint a broader picture of the characters' lives, enhancing the authenticity of the narrative.

The Tapestry of Unity: Diverse Voices

Dialects and vernaculars are not only a tool for historical accuracy but also a means of celebrating diversity within the historical setting. By giving characters from different backgrounds unique voices, you create a rich tapestry of human experience, showcasing the myriad perspectives that contribute to the historical era.

In a story set in a bustling city during the Industrial Revolution, characters from various immigrant communities might bring their unique languages and speech patterns. This diversity reflects the multicultural nature of the city and the interactions between people from different walks of life. Each character's dialect or vernacular becomes a thread in the narrative's fabric, contributing to the vibrant mosaic of the historical setting.

A Mosaic of Authenticity and Artistry

In the grand canvas of historical fiction, dialects and vernaculars are not mere linguistic tools but essential elements that infuse the narrative with authenticity, diversity, and depth. The delicate art of handling these nuances involves diligent research, a balance between authenticity and readability, character consistency, subtle hints, careful word choices, and the unity of diverse voices.

Through dialects and vernaculars, historical fiction becomes a living tapestry, where each character's speech echoes the culture, background, and era they represent. It's an artistic endeavor that transports readers through time, immersing them in the world of the past, evoking the essence of human communication that transcends the boundaries of history.

With a masterful touch, the writer creates a mosaic where authenticity and artistry intertwine, leaving an indelible mark on the reader's heart and mind, reminiscent of a time long gone yet forever alive in the pages of historical fiction.

Chapter 29

Balancing Modern Reader Accessibility with Historical Accuracy

The goal is not only to transport readers to the past but also to engage them in a narrative that resonates with familiarity. Achieving this balance requires a blend of artistry, research, and a keen understanding of the needs and expectations of today's readers. One of the challenges in historical fiction lies in the language used by characters. While authentic dialogue from the era may enhance historical accuracy, it can also alienate modern readers. Strive for a balance where the dialogue reflects the era's essence while remaining intelligible to contemporary readers.

Consider using a slightly modernized version of historical language to retain the flavor of the time while eliminating archaic terms or sentence structures that might hinder readability. Employ familiar language with the occasional insertion of era-specific words or expressions. This approach maintains accessibility without diluting the historical atmosphere.

Despite the temporal gulf, the emotions, desires, and conflicts that drive characters remain universally relatable. The struggles of love, ambition, loss, and self-discovery transcend time. Creating characters with whom modern readers can empathize bridges the gap between eras, fostering a connection that goes beyond historical context.

Embed modern sensibilities in your characters' emotional journeys. While their actions may be guided by the values of the past, their inner struggles can mirror contemporary human experiences. This relatability enhances reader engagement, allowing them to navigate the historical landscape through characters they understand and care about.

Societal norms and expectations vary across eras. To balance modern accessibility with historical accuracy, provide context for unfamiliar customs and behaviors. While you strive to avoid lengthy exposition, strategic integration of explanations or character observations can elucidate the nuances of the time without interrupting the narrative flow.

For instance, if your story is set in a time when women's rights were limited, introduce a character who questions or challenges these norms. This character can act as a bridge, allowing modern readers to view the era through a lens of questioning and growth while preserving historical authenticity.

Visual and sensory details play a pivotal role in transporting readers to a different era. These details, when meticulously crafted, enable readers to visualize the settings, clothing, and ambiance of the past. Strive for a balance that evokes the historical context without overwhelming readers with exhaustive descriptions.

Integrate visual and sensory cues in a way that immerses readers in the world of the story. A well-placed detail about the texture of a fabric, the scent of a flower, or the taste of a dish can evoke the atmosphere of the past without slowing down the narrative. These subtle touches become the connective tissue that weaves historical authenticity into the tapestry of modern accessibility.

While historical fiction thrives on the portrayal of a specific era, it also provides an opportunity to explore themes that resonate with readers across time. Themes of love, power, identity, and the search for meaning are threads that weave through the fabric of human existence regardless of the historical backdrop.

Infuse these universal themes into your narrative, allowing characters to grapple with questions and challenges that mirror the human experience. By weaving these threads into the historical context, you create a narrative that bridges the temporal gap, inviting readers to reflect on their own lives while journeying through the past.

As the writer, you act as a mediator between eras, using your craft to seamlessly guide readers from the present into the past. Employ narrative techniques that provide context, explanations, and emotional resonance, making the historical landscape accessible without compromising its authenticity.

Strategically use introspection, dialogue, and interactions to unveil the era's intricacies. Allow characters to question, compare, and react to their surroundings, offering readers a lens through which they can explore the unfamiliar terrain of history. By balancing the role of the writer as a mediator, you foster a connection between readers and characters that spans centuries.

As you refine your manuscript, pay special attention to the interplay between modern accessibility and historical accuracy. During the editing process, assess each element— dialogue, setting, character dynamics—for its contribution to both authenticity and reader engagement. Trim any excesses that might detract from the narrative's flow or comprehension, ensuring that every element serves the dual purpose of immersing readers in the era while captivating their interest.

Seek feedback from beta readers or critique partners who can provide insights from both a historical and modern perspective. Their perspectives can help you refine the balance, fine-tuning the narrative to create a seamless fusion of past and present.

The delicate balance between modern accessibility and historical accuracy is an intricate dance. It requires a symphony of research, character relatability, context, sensory details, universal themes, and the skilled hand of editing. When executed with care, this harmonious blend transports readers through time, creating a narrative that bridges the gap between eras while captivating the hearts and minds of modern audiences. The result is a masterpiece that honors the past, engages the present, and leaves a lasting legacy in the annals of historical fiction.

Chapter 30
Navigating Cultural Sensitivities

Both Harper Lee and Toni Morrison are esteemed authors who navigated cultural sensitivities with remarkable skill in their works, especially in dealing with historically diverse and thematically charged fiction. Their novels, "To Kill a Mockingbird" by Harper Lee and various works by Toni Morrison, such as "Beloved" and "The Bluest Eye," tackle challenging topics with depth, empathy, and a commitment to exploring the complex layers of society. Let's delve into how each of these extraordinary authors managed cultural sensitivities while crafting emotionally charged plots.

Harper Lee and "To Kill a Mockingbird"

"To Kill a Mockingbird" is a timeless classic that confronts themes of racial injustice, inequality, and moral dilemmas within the setting of a small Southern town during the 1930s. Harper Lee masterfully navigates these sensitive issues by weaving them into a compelling narrative that revolves around the experiences of Scout Finch, her brother Jem, and their father Atticus.

1. **Empathetic Characterization**: Lee creates characters that embody the diverse perspectives and experiences of the time. Atticus Finch, a principled lawyer defending a black man accused of raping a white woman, is a symbol of moral integrity. Scout and Jem, as young observers, provide a lens through which readers can explore the complexities of racism, social norms, and empathy.

2. **Humanizing the Struggle**: The novel humanizes the struggle against racism by depicting the resilience and strength of its black characters, particularly Calpurnia and Tom Robinson. It also portrays the devastating consequences of racism on both the oppressed and the oppressors, illustrating the destructiveness of prejudice.

3. **The Power of Innocence**: Through the eyes of Scout, a young girl grappling with the complexities of the adult world, Lee offers a perspective that resonates with readers of all ages. Scout's innocence serves as a powerful contrast to the bigotry she encounters, inviting readers to reflect on the profound impact of prejudice on young minds.

4. **Historical Context**: Lee grounds her narrative in the historical context of the Great Depression and the racially charged atmosphere of the South. This setting allows her to explore the deeply ingrained prejudices of the era, shedding light on the systemic issues that shaped society.

5. **Balancing Hope and Reality**: Lee doesn't shy away from the harsh realities of racial injustice, but she also weaves threads of hope and resilience throughout the novel. The character of Atticus Finch represents the possibility of change and justice, even in the face of overwhelming adversity.

6. **Respectful Language**: While using language that reflects the racial attitudes of the time, Lee ensures that her characters' dialogue and narrative language remain respectful and sensitive. This approach acknowledges the historical context while avoiding

gratuitous or offensive language.

By addressing these themes through the lens of empathy, historical context, and the universal experiences of childhood, Harper Lee navigates the cultural sensitivities inherent in discussing racial inequality and moral challenges.

Toni Morrison and Exploring the Black Experience

Toni Morrison is renowned for her powerful exploration of the African American experience, tackling themes such as identity, trauma, legacy, and the impact of history on the present. Her novels, including "Beloved" and "The Bluest Eye," demonstrate a nuanced approach to cultural sensitivities, rooted in a deep understanding of the complexities of race and identity.

1. **Rich Character Development**: Morrison's characters are multi-dimensional, reflecting the intricacies of the black experience. She humanizes her characters, providing them with unique voices, backgrounds, and motivations. Through their perspectives, readers gain insight into the challenges, joys, and struggles faced by African Americans.

2. **Historical Resonance**: Morrison's works often draw on historical events and the legacy of slavery, creating a bridge between the past and the present. This historical resonance allows her to explore the lasting impact of systemic injustices while emphasizing the importance of confronting and acknowledging that history.

3. **Symbolism and Allegory**: Morrison employs symbolism and allegory to convey profound messages. In "Beloved," the character of Beloved herself is a

powerful symbol, representing the haunting legacy of slavery. This approach allows Morrison to explore the emotional and psychological dimensions of her characters' experiences.

4. **Language and Authenticity**: Morrison's language is evocative, lyrical, and steeped in the cultural nuances of the African American community. Her use of language captures the beauty, pain, and richness of her characters' lives. She doesn't shy away from using dialects or vernacular when appropriate, enhancing the authenticity of her storytelling.

5. **Balancing Empowerment and Vulnerability**: Morrison's characters often exhibit strength and resilience in the face of adversity, but they are also allowed moments of vulnerability. This balance allows readers to connect with the characters on a deeply human level, transcending racial boundaries.

6. **Community and Relationships**: Morrison's novels often emphasize the importance of community, family, and the relationships that sustain individuals through challenging times. This focus on human connections underscores the universality of her themes.

By weaving together history, symbolism, authentic language, and rich characters, Toni Morrison creates narratives that confront cultural sensitivities with nuance and depth. Her exploration of the African American experience resonates with readers while fostering understanding and empathy.

Empathy, Depth, and Cultural Sensitivity

Both Harper Lee and Toni Morrison exemplify how to navigate cultural sensitivities while crafting emotionally charged historical fiction. Their approaches include empathetic character development, historical context, a respectful language, symbolism, and a deep understanding of the human experience. By balancing modern accessibility with historical accuracy, they invite readers to engage with challenging themes, fostering dialogue and understanding. Their masterful storytelling serves as a beacon, guiding writers to tackle complex issues while respecting the sensitivities of diverse readerships.

Chapter 31
Respectful Portrayals of Diverse Cultures

Crafting a plotline in historical fiction that respectfully portrays diverse cultures requires a combination of research, empathy, sensitivity, and a commitment to authenticity. It's essential to approach the portrayal of different cultures with the utmost respect, avoiding stereotypes, and striving to represent the complexities, strengths, and challenges of each culture. Here are some guidelines to create a respectful portrayal of diverse cultures in your historical fiction plotline:

1. **Thorough Research**: Dive deep into the history, customs, traditions, and social dynamics of the cultures you intend to portray. This research should encompass both the historical context and the specific time period in which your story is set. Understand the cultural nuances, values, and perspectives of the people you are depicting.

2. **Multiple Perspectives**: Incorporate diverse characters from the cultures you're representing, allowing readers to see the variety of experiences within a given culture. Avoid presenting a monolithic view of any culture, as this oversimplification can reinforce stereotypes.

3. **Complex Characters**: Develop well-rounded characters from diverse backgrounds. They should have individual motivations, strengths, weaknesses, and unique voices. Avoid reducing characters to mere representatives of their culture; instead, showcase the depth of their personalities.

4. **Avoid Stereotypes**: Steer clear of cultural stereotypes, which can perpetuate bias and misrepresentation. Each culture is rich and multifaceted, and it's essential to portray its diversity accurately. Challenge your own assumptions and biases during the writing process.

5. **Consult Experts**: If possible, seek guidance from individuals who belong to the cultures you're depicting. Sensitivity readers or cultural consultants can provide invaluable insights, helping you navigate potential pitfalls and ensuring that your portrayal is respectful and accurate.

6. **Portray Real Challenges**: Acknowledge the challenges and adversities faced by characters from diverse cultures. Highlight their resilience and strength, but also show how systemic issues and historical context may have impacted their lives.

7. **Cultural Context**: Situate your characters within their cultural context. Show how historical events, societal norms, and the cultural landscape influenced their actions, decisions, and interactions. This helps readers understand the reasons behind characters' behaviors.

8. **Empathy and Authenticity**: Approach the portrayal of diverse cultures with empathy and authenticity. Your goal is to create a genuine and respectful representation that resonates with readers while honoring the cultural experiences you're depicting.

9. **Highlight Shared Humanity**: Emphasize the shared human experiences that transcend cultural boundaries. Themes like love, friendship, family, and the pursuit of happiness are universal, and they can serve as bridges between cultures.

10. **Promote Understanding**: Use your plotline as an opportunity to foster understanding, empathy, and cross-cultural dialogue. Address the common ground that can be found among diverse cultures, as well as the potential for growth and positive change through interactions with characters from different backgrounds.

11. **Be Open to Feedback**: Be receptive to feedback from beta readers, sensitivity readers, or anyone who can provide insights into the portrayal of diverse cultures. Constructive criticism can help you refine your representation and ensure that it aligns with the principles of respect and authenticity.

By following these guidelines, you can create a plotline in historical fiction that not only respects diverse cultures but also enriches the narrative with depth, authenticity, and a celebration of the shared human experience. Your commitment to respectful portrayal will resonate with readers and contribute to a more inclusive literary landscape.

Chapter 32
Using Symbolism and Themes in Historical Fiction

Where the past and imagination intertwine, lies a profound art—the art of weaving symbols and themes into the narrative tapestry. Through the skillful integration of symbols and the exploration of universal themes, historical fiction gains depth, resonance, and the power to transcend time. In this exploration, we delve into the nuanced techniques that elevate historical fiction, transforming it into a rich and meaningful journey through history, culture, and the human experience.

Symbols: The Language of Metaphors

Symbols are the silent eloquence of historical fiction, resonating with layers of meaning that evoke emotions, invite reflection, and bind readers to the narrative. They transcend mere objects or events, becoming vessels of significance that enrich the storytelling. When used with finesse, symbols become a bridge connecting the past with the present, allowing readers to engage with the story on a profound level.

1. **Research-Infused Symbolism**: Root symbols in the historical context of the era you're portraying. Draw from the culture, beliefs, and events of the time. A symbol that holds meaning in one era might have a completely different significance in another. For instance, a specific flower might represent love in one period and mourning in another, reflecting the shifting cultural landscape.

2. **Universal Resonance**: Choose symbols with

universal resonance. Symbols that tap into the fundamental aspects of the human experience—love, loss, freedom, identity—transcend time and cultural boundaries, making them accessible and relatable to modern readers. These symbols invite readers to connect with the historical narrative on a personal level, fostering empathy and emotional engagement.

3. **Subtle Foreshadowing**: Employ symbols as subtle foreshadowing devices. A recurring symbol can foreshadow significant events or character arcs, adding an element of anticipation and intrigue. A symbolic object introduced early in the story may gain heightened meaning as the plot unfolds, leaving readers with a sense of discovery and interconnectedness.

4. **Character-Centric Symbolism**: Assign specific symbols to characters, aligning them with their personality, journey, or role in the narrative. A character's relationship with a symbol can evolve, reflecting their growth or transformation. This personalized symbolism adds depth to character development and allows readers to explore the intricacies of individual experiences.

5. **Narrative Thread**: Integrate symbols as a thread that weaves through the entire narrative. This unifying element creates a sense of cohesion, connecting disparate events, characters, and themes. The recurring presence of a symbol becomes a point of focus, inviting readers to unravel its significance and its evolving role in the story.

6. **Layered Interpretations**: Encourage multiple interpretations of symbols. A well-crafted symbol is open to various layers of meaning, allowing readers to

derive insights that resonate with their own experiences, perspectives, and emotions. This complexity invites discussion and fosters a deeper connection between readers and the narrative.

Themes: The Threads of Meaning

Themes in historical fiction are the threads of meaning that run through the tapestry of the narrative. They encompass the fundamental ideas, questions, and concepts that shape the story's essence, offering readers a lens through which to explore the historical era and the human condition. By intertwining themes with historical context, characters, and events, historical fiction gains a timeless quality that transcends its setting.

1. **Historical Context**: Themes should harmonize with the historical context of the era you're portraying. Explore the prevalent ideas, ideologies, and conflicts of the time, allowing them to inform the themes of your narrative. This alignment enhances the authenticity of the story, providing readers with a deeper understanding of the historical period.

2. **Character Journeys**: Themes should resonate with the characters' journeys, motivating their actions, decisions, and growth. The exploration of a theme can mirror a character's personal development, presenting opportunities for reflection, transformation, and self-discovery. A character's relationship with a theme can evolve, adding layers of complexity to their arc.

3. **Contrasting Themes**: Introduce contrasting themes that reflect the complexities of the historical era and the characters' experiences. These opposing ideas

create tension, allowing readers to navigate the gray areas of morality, society, and individual choices. The interplay between contrasting themes adds depth to the narrative, sparking discussion and contemplation.

4. **Universal Human Experience**: Infuse themes that resonate with the universal aspects of the human experience. Themes such as love, power, identity, justice, and resilience are timeless, transcending historical boundaries. When readers recognize these universal themes, they find a common ground with characters from the past, forging a connection that bridges the temporal gap.

5. **Cultural Nuances**: Acknowledge the cultural nuances of the historical period and the characters' backgrounds. Themes may be influenced by cultural beliefs, social norms, and the specific challenges faced by individuals from diverse cultures. This recognition adds layers of authenticity and allows readers to appreciate the intricacies of cultural experiences.

6. **Emotional Resonance**: Themes should evoke emotional responses from readers. Whether it's empathy, introspection, outrage, or hope, the exploration of themes should leave a lasting impact, prompting readers to reflect on their own lives, beliefs, and values. The emotional resonance of themes is what lingers in the hearts of readers long after they've turned the last page.

The Harmonious Interplay: Symbols and Themes

The true magic of historical fiction emerges when symbols and themes intertwine, creating a harmonious interplay that elevates the narrative to a higher plane of meaning. As you craft your historical fiction plotline, consider the ways in which symbols and themes can complement each other, enriching the story's depth and significance.

1. **Symbolic Themes**: Explore themes through the use of symbols, allowing these tangible representations to convey the essence of the themes. A recurring symbol can serve as a visual reminder of the overarching themes, reinforcing their presence throughout the narrative. The symbolism of an object, gesture, or event can encapsulate the thematic undercurrents, inviting readers to unravel their interconnectedness.

2. **Theme-Infused Symbols**: Assign thematic significance to symbols, infusing them with the core ideas and questions that drive the narrative. The symbolic objects or events take on a dual role: they carry the weight of their inherent meaning while also representing the thematic exploration. This layering of symbolism creates a multi-dimensional reading experience.

3. **Enhancing Atmosphere**: Use symbols to enhance the atmosphere and mood of the historical setting. Symbols can evoke the ethos of the era, reinforcing the cultural, emotional, and psychological landscape. Whether it's a symbolic motif that appears in the architecture, clothing, or natural surroundings, these elements contribute to the immersive quality of the historical setting.

4. **Themes in Character Interactions**: Allow themes to shape character interactions, dialogue, and relationships. Characters' beliefs and perspectives may align with or challenge the prevailing themes of the

era. These interactions become vehicles for the exploration and expression of themes, offering readers diverse viewpoints and contributing to the thematic richness of the narrative.

5. **Symbolic Transformation**: Explore the transformation of symbols as characters and the plot evolve. The changing significance of a symbol can mirror the characters' journeys or the shifting dynamics of the historical period. This dynamic transformation of symbols adds a layer of depth, symbolizing the evolution of ideas, values, and human experiences.

6. **The Lingering Echo**: Conclude your historical fiction with a symbolic or thematic resonance that lingers in the minds of readers. The final impression should encapsulate the essence of the narrative, leaving readers with a thought-provoking image, idea, or question. This lingering echo connects the story's themes and symbols, inviting readers to continue their exploration long after the story ends.

An Everlasting Impression

The art of using symbols and themes is a tapestry that enriches the narrative with depth, meaning, and lasting impact. The careful selection and integration of symbols, aligned with universal themes and historical context, elevate the storytelling to a realm where readers are transported through time, cultures, and the human experience. Through this intricate interplay, historical fiction becomes an everlasting impression on the hearts and minds of those who embark on its journey—a testament to the power of symbols and themes in the hands of a skilled storyteller.

Chapter 33
Structuring Your Historical Novel

Where the echoes of the past reverberate through the pages, the structure of a novel is the architect's blueprint, shaping the way readers traverse time, experience cultures, and immerse themselves in bygone eras. Choosing a narrative structure, employing flashbacks and multiple timelines, and adeptly pacing and managing historical details are the hallmarks of a masterful historical novel. This exploration delves into the intricacies of structuring a historical novel, shedding light on the artistry and techniques that create a seamless tapestry of history, emotion, and narrative brilliance.

Choosing a Narrative Structure: Building the Framework

The choice of narrative structure is the foundation upon which the historical novel is built. It dictates the flow of the story, the perspective from which events are unveiled, and the degree of immersion into the historical era. Selecting the right structure is a delicate balance between the demands of the plot, the depth of historical context, and the engagement of the reader.

1. **Linear Chronology**: This straightforward structure unfolds the events of the historical period in a linear fashion. It offers a clear progression of time, allowing readers to follow the characters' journey without major deviations. This structure works well when the historical details and character arcs align harmoniously, and the plot doesn't require significant

shifts in time.

2. **Epistolary Format**: Employing letters, diaries, or other written documents as the narrative backbone lends an intimate and personal touch to the historical novel. The epistolary format allows readers to experience events through the eyes and voices of the characters. It's particularly effective when a deep exploration of characters' thoughts, emotions, and personal experiences is essential to the story.

3. **Multiple Perspectives**: Presenting the historical era from the viewpoints of multiple characters offers a panoramic view of the time period. Each character's perspective brings unique insights, cultural nuances, and personal experiences to the narrative. This structure works well when the historical events impact various characters in distinct ways, allowing readers to witness the era's diversity.

4. **Framed Narrative**: A framed narrative involves a story within a story. It can be a character recounting past events, a discovery of historical artifacts, or a modern-day protagonist uncovering the past. This structure adds layers of depth and intrigue, providing opportunities for parallel narratives and connecting past and present.

5. **Nonlinear Structure**: A non-linear structure employs flashbacks, time jumps, or interwoven timelines to reveal the historical events. This approach creates a sense of mystery and complexity, allowing readers to piece together the historical puzzle. It works well when the plot involves intertwined storylines, secrets from the past, or thematic exploration.

6. **Hybrid Approach**: Often, a combination of narrative

structures can enhance the richness of the historical novel. Combining linear chronology with flashbacks or alternating perspectives can provide a dynamic and layered reading experience, deepening both character development and historical immersion.

Flashbacks and Multiple Timelines: Navigating Time's Currents

Flashbacks and multiple timelines are like portals through which readers can traverse time, gaining insights into the past and the characters' histories. These narrative devices, when used effectively, enhance the complexity of the historical novel, adding depth, context, and a sense of continuity that bridges historical events.

1. **Purposeful Flashbacks**: Flashbacks should serve a clear purpose in the narrative. They can offer backstory, reveal the origins of conflicts, or shed light on the motivations of characters. The key is to ensure that each flashback contributes to the overall plot, character development, or thematic exploration.

2. **Seamless Transitions**: Transitioning between the present narrative and flashbacks requires finesse. Use clear cues, such as chapter breaks, headings, or changes in font style, to indicate shifts in time. Maintain a seamless flow, guiding readers between past and present without causing confusion.

3. **Parallel Timelines**: When employing multiple timelines, consider how they interact and influence each other. Parallel timelines can enhance the sense of mystery, suspense, or interconnectedness in the story. Ensure that each timeline contributes to the overall

narrative arc, allowing readers to uncover the layers of the plot.

4. **Balancing Tension**: Use multiple timelines to create tension and anticipation. Strategic placement of historical events, revelations, or pivotal moments in each timeline can keep readers engaged and eager to uncover the connections between the past and present.

5. **Character Consistency**: Pay attention to character consistency across timelines. Characters should remain true to their personalities, experiences, and motivations, even as they navigate different time periods. This consistency ensures that readers can easily identify and empathize with the characters regardless of the timeline.

6. **Revealing Historical Context**: Through flashbacks and multiple timelines, reveal the historical context organically. Show how past events influence the present, shaping characters, relationships, and societal norms. This layered approach adds depth to the historical setting, allowing readers to understand the roots of the era's challenges and triumphs.

Pacing and Managing Historical Details: Navigating the Past with Precision

Pacing and managing historical details are the compass by which readers navigate the historical novel. Proper pacing ensures that the narrative flows smoothly, maintaining reader engagement, while managing historical details ensures accuracy without overwhelming the story.

1. **Balancing Historical and Emotional Arcs**: Balance the pacing of historical events with the emotional arcs

of the characters. While historical accuracy is essential, the characters' journeys, growth, and conflicts should remain at the forefront. Historical events should serve as a backdrop that enhances character development and thematic exploration.

2. **Selective Details**: Choose historical details that are essential to the plot, themes, or character motivations. Not every historical fact needs extensive exposition. Focus on the details that impact the characters' lives, beliefs, or decisions, providing context without bogging down the narrative.

3. **Immersive Descriptions**: When describing historical settings, use sensory details to immerse readers in the era. Engage the senses, allowing readers to see, hear, smell, and feel the historical environment. This immersion creates a vivid backdrop that enhances the reading experience.

4. **Timing of Information**: Introduce historical details at the right moments in the narrative. Provide the necessary context when it becomes relevant to the characters' experiences or the unfolding plot. Avoid info-dumping or interrupting the flow of the story for extended historical explanations.

5. **Once again - Show, Don't Tell**: Instead of directly stating historical facts, show them through the characters' actions, interactions, and observations. Characters can discuss events, react to societal norms, or confront challenges rooted in the historical context. This approach makes historical details integral to the story, enhancing the reader's understanding.

6. **Research Precision**: Ensure historical accuracy in the details you include. Thorough research is essential to

capture the nuances, customs, and language of the era. However, avoid the temptation to showcase exhaustive research at the expense of the narrative's pacing. Strive for a balance that maintains accuracy while keeping the story engaging.

7. **Reflecting the Time Period**: Use historical details to reflect the time period's values, beliefs, and conflicts. These details should be more than set dressing; they should shape the characters' experiences, decisions, and growth. Historical accuracy extends beyond the surface—it influences the core of the narrative.

A Harmonious Symphony of Structure

The structure of a historical novel is a symphony of choices, carefully composed to transport readers through time, cultures, and the human experience. The narrative structure, the artful use of flashbacks and multiple timelines, and the pacing and management of historical details converge to create a seamless tapestry of history and emotion. The interplay between these elements, when executed with finesse and purpose, elevates the historical novel, leaving readers with a profound sense of connection to the past, a deeper understanding of the present, and a renewed appreciation for the artistry of storytelling.

Chapter 34
Weaving Romance into Historical Fiction

The ability to portray love within the confines of a bygone era, to capture the nuances of relationships in the context of the time, and to balance romantic elements with the grandeur of historical plotlines is the hallmark of a masterful historical romance novelist. This exploration unveils the techniques that breathe life into authentic historical romances, creating narratives that transcend time and touch the hearts of readers.

Writing Authentic Historical Romances: A Journey Through Time

Crafting an authentic historical romance requires a deep understanding of the era you're portraying, as well as a commitment to embracing the cultural norms, societal expectations, and emotional landscapes of the time. Authenticity ensures that the romance feels organic within the historical context, resonating with readers as they journey through a world of bygone days.

Thoroughly research the historical period in which your romance is set. Study the customs, values, and social dynamics of the time, allowing them to shape the interactions and emotions of your characters. By understanding the intricacies of the era, you can infuse authenticity into every aspect of the romance.

Integrate historical details seamlessly into the narrative, enriching the romance with the ambiance and texture of the past. Descriptions of clothing, architecture, food, and cultural practices provide a vivid backdrop, allowing readers to fully immerse themselves in the historical setting.

Pay attention to the language and dialogue of the era. While you don't need to replicate archaic language, infuse a touch of historical flavor into the characters' speech. This adds authenticity to their interactions and reinforces the sense of time and place.

Understand the social expectations and restrictions that governed relationships during the historical period. This knowledge helps you create realistic obstacles and challenges for your characters, driving the tension and emotional depth of the romance.

Recognize that historical romances can encompass diverse backgrounds, experiences, and cultures. Ensure that your portrayal reflects the diversity that existed in the past while remaining sensitive to the historical context and the challenges faced by characters from marginalized communities.

Portraying Relationships in the Context of the Time: Love Across Eras

Portraying relationships authentically within the context of the time period is a delicate balance between historical accuracy and emotional resonance. The dynamics of love, courtship, and intimacy were influenced by societal norms and cultural expectations that vary significantly from contemporary views.

Explore the courtship rituals and traditions of the era. Understand the protocols for introductions, engagements, and the gradual progression of a romantic relationship. Show how characters navigate these customs while expressing their feelings within the boundaries of the time.

Be mindful of the cultural norms and taboos that governed

romantic relationships during the historical period. Characters should navigate these norms, often leading to internal conflicts or external obstacles that enrich the romance.

Examine the chivalrous ideals and gender roles of the time, especially in historical romances set in earlier eras. Highlight the expectations placed on characters based on their gender, while also allowing room for characters who challenge or subvert these roles.

Embrace the emotional subtleties of the time. The expression of emotions, especially love, may be more restrained or conveyed through gestures, glances, or carefully chosen words. Allow the characters to communicate their feelings within the emotional boundaries of the era, allowing readers to appreciate the depth of their connection.

Use the historical context to create unique conflicts and obstacles that test the love between characters. These challenges should stem from the societal norms, class differences, or external events of the era. By intertwining these obstacles with the historical setting, you enhance the complexity of the romance.

Balancing Romantic Elements with Historical Plotlines: The Art of Fusion

A successful historical romance strikes a harmonious balance between romantic elements and the grand sweep of historical plotlines. While the romance forms a central thread, it should seamlessly weave into the broader historical context, enhancing both the love story and the immersive quality of the historical setting.

View the romance and the historical plotlines as intertwined threads. Allow the historical events to influence the romance, shaping the characters' choices, motivations, and personal growth. Conversely, let the romance provide a lens through which readers experience the historical era, revealing its impact on individuals and relationships.

Ensure that the romance aligns with the broader themes of the historical novel. The love story can reflect the era's struggles, societal shifts, or timeless themes that resonate with readers. This thematic resonance adds depth to the romance, elevating it beyond a mere subplot.

Let the characters drive the romance and the historical plotlines. Their goals, conflicts, and emotional journeys should remain at the heart of the narrative. A well-developed romance enhances character development, offering opportunities for growth, introspection, and self-discovery.

Balance the pacing of the romance with the pacing of the historical events. Both elements should complement each other, creating a rhythm that keeps readers engaged. Allow moments of intimacy or emotional connection to unfold at the right moments within the broader context of the plot.

Use the romance to showcase the impact of historical events on individuals and relationships. How do characters respond to societal upheavals, political changes, or cultural shifts? How does their love navigate the challenges brought by the historical context? By intertwining the romance with the historical impact, you create a multidimensional narrative.

A Timeless Fusion

A masterful historical romance is a timeless fusion of love and history, meticulously crafted to transport readers through the corridors of time. By embracing authenticity, portraying relationships within the context of the era, and skillfully balancing romantic elements with the grandeur of historical plotlines, you create a narrative that not only captures the hearts of readers but also paints a vivid portrait of the past. This artful fusion is where the beauty of historical fiction and the power of love converge, leaving readers with a profound connection to both the characters' journey and the echoes of history.

Chapter 35
Creating Historical Villains and Antagonists

Mary Shelley and Bram Stoker, two literary giants of the 19th century, revolutionized the portrayal of villains and antagonists in historical fiction, leaving a lasting impact on the genre. Their masterful craftsmanship in creating authentic villains draws upon historical realities, giving depth and authenticity to their characters.

Mary Shelley's Complex Creations

Mary Shelley's magnum opus, "Frankenstein," published in 1818, is a seminal work of both science fiction and historical fiction. The character of Victor Frankenstein, the ambitious and morally conflicted scientist, is a quintessential example of a villain rooted in historical realities. Shelley weaves a web of ethical dilemmas and societal concerns, reflecting the scientific and philosophical debates of her time.

In the early 19th century, the Age of Enlightenment had given rise to scientific advancements and a fervent pursuit of knowledge. However, this era of progress was also marked by ethical debates about the boundaries of science and the consequences of tampering with nature. Victor Frankenstein's obsessive quest to conquer death and create life reflects the scientific ambitions of the era, but it also serves as a cautionary tale about the unchecked pursuit of knowledge.

Victor's transformation from a curious and driven young man to a tormented and morally questionable figure is a testament to Shelley's exploration of the ethical ramifications of scientific progress. The hubris of Victor, driven by his desire to play god, leads to tragedy and destruction, mirroring the fears of the time regarding the consequences of unchecked scientific experimentation.

Additionally, Shelley's incorporation of the Romantic era's fascination with the sublime—a concept that combines awe and terror—adds another layer to the portrayal of the villain. Victor's creation, often referred to as "the monster," embodies both the sublime and the tragic. His isolation, rejection, and longing for acceptance create a poignant narrative of human suffering and the consequences of societal prejudices. This portrayal of the monster adds complexity to the villain, blurring the lines between good and evil, and forcing readers to confront the societal factors that contributed to his descent into violence.

Through Victor Frankenstein and his creation, Mary Shelley crafted a villain deeply rooted in the historical realities and ethical debates of her time. She masterfully blended scientific ambition, the dangers of unchecked knowledge, and societal fears into a compelling antagonist that continues to captivate readers and challenge their understanding of good and evil.

Bram Stoker's Alluring Darkness

Bram Stoker's "Dracula," published in 1897, introduced one of the most iconic villains in literary history—Count Dracula, a timeless embodiment of evil, rooted in historical and cultural contexts. Stoker's portrayal of the vampire count is a masterstroke of character development, exploring the allure of darkness and the fear of the unknown.

Count Dracula, a Transylvanian nobleman with a thirst for blood and an ability to manipulate the minds of his victims, is a compelling antagonist that draws upon historical legends, cultural anxieties, and the fascination with the supernatural prevalent in the Victorian era.

Stoker's choice to set part of the novel in the distant, mysterious land of Transylvania adds an air of exoticism and otherness to the character of Dracula. The portrayal of Eastern Europe as a place shrouded in superstition and ancient traditions plays on the fears and prejudices of Western European readers. The contrast between the modern, rational world of London and the ancient, eerie landscapes of Transylvania heightens the sense of danger and the unknown.

Additionally, Stoker tapped into the anxieties of his time, where scientific advancements and the spread of knowledge clashed with the lingering shadows of the past. The late 19th century was a period of rapid change, with advancements in medicine, technology, and exploration. However, there was also a fear of the dark forces that science couldn't explain— the fear of the supernatural and the uncharted territories of the human psyche.

Dracula's ability to control minds, transform into various forms, and exert power over the forces of nature taps into these fears, creating a villain who embodies the unknown and challenges the boundaries of human understanding. Furthermore, the theme of blood, central to the novel, is both a symbol of life and a potent element of horror, connecting Dracula to ancient fears and taboos.

Stoker's portrayal of Dracula as a charismatic and seductive figure adds another layer of complexity to the character. Dracula's allure is rooted in the concept of the "Byronic hero," a romantic archetype characterized by its mysterious and dark attractiveness. This allure makes Dracula not just a terrifying villain but also a magnetic and enigmatic presence.

Through Count Dracula, Bram Stoker delves into the historical and cultural fears of his time, tapping into the allure of the unknown, the clash between science and superstition, and the fascination with the dark and enigmatic. The character of Dracula has become an immortal representation of evil, rooted in the historical and psychological anxieties of the Victorian era.

Developing Multi-dimensional Antagonists

One of the remarkable qualities shared by Mary Shelley and Bram Stoker is their ability to create multi-dimensional antagonists—villains with layers, motivations, and complexities that transcend the traditional notions of good and evil.

The Layers of Victor Frankenstein

Victor Frankenstein, the central character in Shelley's "Frankenstein," is a prime example of a multi-dimensional antagonist. While he may be seen as the creator of the monster, his own actions and moral struggles position him as a complex figure with both admirable traits and fatal flaws.

Victor's initial motivations are driven by a thirst for knowledge and the desire to conquer death. He is portrayed as a brilliant and ambitious young scientist, eager to push the boundaries of human understanding. His relentless pursuit of his goals, while admirable in its determination, blinds him to the potential consequences of his actions.

As the narrative unfolds, it becomes evident that Victor is not a malevolent villain in the traditional sense. His creation, often referred to as "the monster," is a reflection of Victor's own ambitions, his disregard for ethical considerations, and his inability to take responsibility for his actions. The monster's suffering, isolation, and longing for acceptance paint a sympathetic picture, forcing readers to question the true source of evil in the story.

Victor's internal struggle adds depth to his character. He grapples with guilt, remorse, and the realization that his actions have brought misery to those around him. He is tormented by the consequences of his creation, highlighting the ethical dilemmas inherent in scientific progress and the responsibilities of those who wield knowledge.

Furthermore, Victor's interactions with the monster reveal a complex dynamic. While he initially rejects his creation, he later recognizes the monster's humanity and the role he played in the creature's suffering. This realization humanizes Victor, blurring the lines between antagonist and protagonist, and emphasizing the shared responsibility for the tragedy that unfolds.

Mary Shelley's portrayal of Victor Frankenstein as a multi-dimensional antagonist challenges the traditional notions of villainy. He is a character with virtues, flaws, and moral struggles, making him a compelling figure whose actions and decisions drive the narrative, while also serving as a cautionary example of the consequences of unchecked ambition.

The Enigmatic Nature of Count Dracula

Bram Stoker's Count Dracula, the eponymous antagonist in "Dracula," is another exemplary multi-dimensional villain. His character is a masterful blend of ancient evil, supernatural allure, and a tragic history that evokes both fear and sympathy.

Dracula's centuries-long existence adds a layer of historical depth to his character. He is portrayed as a creature of ancient lineage, rooted in the folklore and legends of Eastern Europe. This historical connection, combined with his ability to manipulate and control, gives him a sense of power that transcends time.

However, Dracula is not merely a one-dimensional embodiment of evil. Stoker provides glimpses into his tragic past, revealing the loneliness and suffering that accompany his immortality. His motivation to leave his homeland and seek new territories is born out of survival and a desire for a fresh start. This complexity adds a layer of empathy, inviting readers to question whether Dracula's actions are solely the result of malevolence or a desperate struggle for existence.

Furthermore, Dracula's allure is a central aspect of his character. He is depicted as charismatic, seductive, and capable of exerting control over others. His ability to charm and manipulate draws parallels with the concept of the "seductive villain," a character who lures others into darkness. This duality—his terrifying nature as a vampire and his seductive charisma—creates a fascinating tension that defines his interactions with other characters.

Stoker's decision to allow Dracula to express himself through letters and journals adds another layer of complexity to his character. Through these personal accounts, readers gain insight into Dracula's thoughts, motivations, and the loneliness that comes with his immortal existence. This narrative choice humanizes the villain, blurring the lines between good and evil and prompting readers to consider the tragedy inherent in his story.

The multi-dimensional nature of Count Dracula, with his historical origins, tragic past, seductive allure, and enigmatic personality, makes him a timeless antagonist that defies simple categorization. He is a character whose complexity challenges readers to confront the nuances of good and evil, inviting empathy even as he instills fear.

The Role of Evil in Historical Narratives

Both Mary Shelley and Bram Stoker use the concept of evil as a powerful narrative tool in their historical fiction. Evil, whether personified in a character or depicted as a pervasive force, serves as a catalyst for exploration, a reflection of societal anxieties, and a source of thematic depth.

The Dual Nature of Evil in "Frankenstein"

In "Frankenstein," Mary Shelley explores the dual nature of evil, showcasing how it can arise from both external sources and internal choices. The character of the monster embodies this duality, as he is both a victim of external rejection and a product of Victor Frankenstein's ambitious and unchecked actions.

The societal rejection the monster faces plays a significant role in shaping his path. From the moment of his creation, he is met with fear, disgust, and violence, leading to his isolation and loneliness. This treatment pushes him to the margins of society, and he responds with anger and a desire for revenge.

However, it is essential to recognize that the monster's initial intentions are not inherently evil. He longs for acceptance, companionship, and understanding, reflecting the basic human need for connection. It is only when he realizes that his appearance ensures perpetual rejection that he turns to violence and revenge, a response born out of the cruelty he has endured.

On the other hand, Victor Frankenstein's actions represent another form of evil—the unchecked pursuit of knowledge without regard for the consequences. His ambition, fueled by a desire to overcome death, leads him to engage in unethical experiments and ultimately creates the monster. Victor's refusal to take responsibility for his creation and his failure to provide the monster with companionship contribute to the tragedy that unfolds.

Shelley's exploration of evil in "Frankenstein" challenges the notion of a purely malevolent antagonist. The monster's actions, while horrific, are rooted in a deep sense of abandonment and the search for meaning. Victor, despite his admirable qualities, becomes a source of evil through his recklessness and neglect.

This dual nature of evil serves as a cautionary tale about the moral consequences of human actions. Shelley's narrative prompts readers to consider the roles of responsibility, empathy, and the impact of societal rejection on the path individuals choose. Through the intertwining stories of the monster and Victor, she reveals the complexity of evil, showing how it can arise from external circumstances and internal choices.

The Enduring Power of Evil in "Dracula"

In "Dracula," Bram Stoker uses the concept of evil as an enduring and pervasive force, intertwining it with the supernatural and the historical. Count Dracula, as the embodiment of evil, represents an ancient darkness that spans centuries, defying time and cultural boundaries.

Dracula's status as a vampire, a creature that thrives on the lifeblood of others, connects him to the concept of the undead, a symbolic representation of the persistence of evil even beyond death. His immortality allows him to traverse generations, adapting to the changing world while remaining a constant source of fear and malevolence.

Furthermore, the historical context of the novel plays a

significant role in shaping the portrayal of evil. Stoker draws upon the anxieties of the Victorian era, where scientific advancements and a clash between modernity and the past were prominent themes. The juxtaposition of London's rational and technologically advanced society with the ancient, mystical landscapes of Transylvania emphasizes the collision between progress and the unknown.

Dracula's ability to manipulate and control the minds of his victims adds another layer to the concept of evil. He exerts a psychological hold on those he preys upon, symbolizing the insidious nature of malevolence. This power over the human psyche taps into the fears of the era—fears of the unknown, the uncontrollable, and the loss of one's individuality.

Moreover, the allure of darkness, the seductive nature of evil, is a recurring theme in the novel. Dracula's ability to charm and manipulate draws from the concept of the "seductive villain," a character who uses charm and charisma to lure others into darkness. This seductive allure complicates the portrayal of evil, blurring the lines between villainy and attraction.

Through Count Dracula, Bram Stoker explores the enduring and multifaceted nature of evil, a force that spans centuries, adapts to cultural shifts, and draws from the fears and anxieties of its time. The supernatural and historical dimensions of Dracula's character make him a formidable antagonist, serving as a representation of ancient malevolence that continues to captivate readers across generations.

The Legacy of Authentic Villains and Antagonists

Mary Shelley and Bram Stoker, through their masterful creations of Victor Frankenstein and Count Dracula, respectively, established a legacy of authentic villains and multi-dimensional antagonists in the realm of historical fiction. These characters transcend simple notions of good and evil, embodying the complexities, fears, and ethical dilemmas of their respective eras. Shelley and Stoker's portrayal of villains rooted in historical realities, their development of multi-dimensional antagonists, and their exploration of the role of evil in historical narratives set a standard for the genre, inspiring generations of writers to craft compelling characters that continue to resonate with readers and challenge our understanding of humanity and the past.

Chapter 36
Tackling Battles and Wars

Historical fiction serves as a gateway to the past, transporting readers to eras of great conflicts and monumental events. Authors like Bernard Cornwell and Leo Tolstoy have demonstrated an unparalleled ability to craft authentic battle scenes that bring these historical conflicts to life. Through accurate depictions of historical conflicts, skillful writing of action scenes in historical context, and the art of conveying the emotional impact of war, these authors have woven tapestries of realism and emotion that resonate with readers, immersing them in the tumultuous world of warfare.

Accurate Depictions of Historical Conflicts: Capturing the Essence of War

One of the hallmarks of great historical fiction is its ability to capture the essence of historical conflicts, accurately portraying the strategies, tactics, and visceral experiences of warfare. Bernard Cornwell, known for his masterful series of historical novels, has adeptly navigated the terrain of various eras, creating vivid battle scenes that transport readers to the heart of combat.

Cornwell's "The Saxon Stories" series, set during the Viking Age, exemplifies his commitment to historical accuracy in depicting battles. The author's meticulous research shines through as he describes the formations of shield walls, the clash of weapons, and the chaos of the battlefield. By incorporating historical details, such as the types of weaponry, the role of shield bearers, and the tactics employed by Viking warriors, Cornwell immerses readers in the authenticity of the era.

Similarly, Leo Tolstoy's monumental work, "War and Peace," stands as a testament to the power of accurate historical depictions. Set against the backdrop of the Napoleonic Wars, the novel weaves a tapestry of war, love, and society. Tolstoy's descriptions of the battles, particularly the Battle of Borodino, showcase his attention to historical detail. His portrayal of the chaos, the impact of artillery, and the sheer scale of the conflict captures the essence of the era's warfare.

Both Cornwell and Tolstoy recognize the importance of understanding the historical context in which battles occurred. They meticulously research the weapons, tactics, and strategies of the time, ensuring that their descriptions align with historical realities. By doing so, they create battle scenes that not only engage readers but also educate them about the intricacies of historical warfare.

Writing Action Scenes in Historical Context: A Symphony of Movement and Strategy

Crafting action scenes in a historical context requires a delicate balance between the visceral immediacy of battle and the strategic nuances that shaped the outcomes of conflicts. Bernard Cornwell and Leo Tolstoy navigate this balance with finesse, breathing life into their narratives by interweaving dynamic action with the strategic elements that defined historical warfare.

Cornwell's portrayal of battle scenes often incorporates a deep understanding of military strategy and tactics. His characters engage in skirmishes and clashes, but these actions are not mere chaotic brawls. Instead, they are informed by the knowledge of formations, terrain, and the strengths and weaknesses of the opposing forces. This strategic layer adds depth to the action, immersing readers in the calculated decisions that shaped the course of battle.

In "The Saxon Stories," the character Uhtred, a warrior shaped by the tumultuous events of 9th-century England, serves as a conduit for Cornwell's exploration of battle strategy. Uhtred's knowledge of shield walls, flanking maneuvers, and the importance of terrain reflects the historical context in which he operates. Through Uhtred's perspective, Cornwell educates readers about the tactics of the time, enhancing the authenticity of the narrative.

Tolstoy, in "War and Peace," takes a different approach to action scenes. While his battle descriptions do convey the chaos and immediacy of combat, he also uses these scenes to examine the broader philosophical and historical aspects of war. The Battle of Borodino, a central event in the novel, serves as a canvas for Tolstoy to explore the futility of war, the role of fate, and the impact of historical forces on individual lives.

Tolstoy's focus on the human experience within the context of battle creates a poignant contrast to the grand scale of historical events. He delves into the thoughts and emotions of his characters, capturing their fears, courage, and moments of introspection amid the chaos of war. Through this approach, Tolstoy adds a layer of humanity to the action scenes, making them resonate on a deeply emotional level.

Both Cornwell and Tolstoy recognize that action scenes are not just about the clash of weapons but also about the strategic decisions that shaped conflicts and the impact of these battles on the lives of individuals. By seamlessly weaving together movement, strategy, and emotional resonance, they create action scenes that are both historically informed and emotionally compelling.

Conveying the Emotional Impact of War: From Courage to Tragedy

The emotional impact of war is a central theme in historical fiction, and authors like Bernard Cornwell and Leo Tolstoy excel in conveying the complex array of emotions that arise in the midst of conflict. Through their characters, these authors explore the spectrum of human experiences, from courage and camaraderie to tragedy and loss.

Cornwell's characters often find themselves in the crucible of war, facing daunting odds and the ever-present specter of death. Yet, within this grim reality, there is a profound sense of camaraderie and loyalty that emerges. Cornwell's characters forge bonds on the battlefield, standing shoulder to shoulder against the chaos. This sense of brotherhood, born out of shared danger, adds a layer of emotional depth to his battle scenes.

The character of Richard Sharpe, Cornwell's iconic soldier in the "Sharpe" series, exemplifies the courage and resilience of individuals in the face of historical conflicts. Sharpe's determination, resourcefulness, and unwavering commitment to his fellow soldiers make him a compelling figure in the midst of battle. Through Sharpe's experiences, readers witness the emotional fortitude required to confront the horrors of war.

Tolstoy, in "War and Peace," takes a more introspective approach to the emotional impact of war. He explores the psychological toll of conflict on his characters, delving into their fears, doubts, and moments of existential reflection. The Battle of Borodino, with its devastation and loss of life, becomes a canvas for Tolstoy to examine the futility of war and the unpredictable nature of destiny.

The character of Prince Andrei Bolkonsky, who undergoes a

transformation after being wounded in the battle, embodies the emotional upheaval brought about by war. His introspective journey, marked by disillusionment and a search for meaning, serves as a poignant exploration of the human psyche in the midst of historical turmoil. Tolstoy's ability to convey the inner struggles of his characters adds a layer of emotional richness to the narrative.

In both authors' works, the emotional impact of war extends beyond the battlefield, affecting the lives of characters long after the conflict has ended. The scars of war—physical, emotional, and psychological—linger, shaping the trajectories of individuals and societies. By exploring the emotional aftermath of war, Cornwell and Tolstoy create narratives that resonate with readers, inviting them to contemplate the profound human cost of historical conflicts.

Crafting Authentic Battle Scenes with Historical Resonance

Bernard Cornwell and Leo Tolstoy, each in their unique style, have demonstrated the art of creating authentic battle scenes in historical fiction. Through accurate depictions of historical conflicts, the careful weaving of action scenes within historical context, and the skillful conveyance of the emotional impact of war, these authors have brought the past to life, allowing readers to experience the tumultuous world of historical warfare.

Cornwell's attention to historical accuracy, coupled with his focus on strategic details, immerses readers in the historical realities of battles. His characters, shaped by the conflicts they face, forge emotional connections that resonate with readers, reminding them of the camaraderie and courage that emerge in the crucible of war.

Tolstoy, on the other hand, explores the philosophical and emotional dimensions of war, using battle scenes as a canvas for broader themes. His characters grapple with the futility of conflict, the role of fate, and the enduring impact of historical forces. Tolstoy's introspective approach captures the psychological toll of war, allowing readers to witness the inner struggles of his characters.

In the hands of these masterful authors, battle scenes become more than mere descriptions of combat. They serve as windows into historical eras, offering insights into the strategies, emotions, and human experiences that shaped conflicts. Through their craft, Cornwell and Tolstoy have crafted authentic battle scenes that stand as powerful testaments to the complex tapestry of historical fiction, enriching the genre and leaving a lasting impact on readers.

Chapter 37
Editing and Revising Historical Fiction

To create a compelling historical narrative, authors must not only craft a captivating story but also fine-tune their work to ensure historical authenticity. Addressing anachronisms and inconsistencies, fine-tuning historical accuracy, and seeking feedback from historical experts are essential steps in the editing and revision process. By mastering these aspects, authors can elevate their historical novels to a professional level, creating works that transport readers to the past while resonating with the present.

Addressing Anachronisms and Inconsistencies: Preserving the Historical Fabric

Anachronisms, those chronological inconsistencies that disrupt the historical integrity of a novel, can be jarring for readers and undermine the immersive experience of historical fiction. Careful editing and revision are essential to identify and eliminate anachronistic elements, preserving the coherence of the historical fabric.

The first step in addressing anachronisms is a thorough review of details. Examine the language, clothing, technology, customs, and societal norms presented in the narrative. Check for anachronistic words or phrases that did not exist during the historical period. Ensure that characters' actions and interactions are in alignment with the beliefs and practices of the time.

Additionally, pay attention to anachronistic concepts or events. Historical fiction requires authors to respect the boundaries of the era they are portraying. Avoid projecting modern sensibilities onto historical characters. Be mindful of historical events that may not have occurred or had a different context during the period. If there are references to events that took place after the setting of the novel, consider revising or recontextualizing them to maintain historical accuracy.

The consistency of historical details is equally crucial. Ensure that the rules and norms established within the historical world of the novel remain consistent throughout the narrative. A sudden deviation from historical accuracy can disrupt the reader's immersion and detract from the authenticity of the story.

The editing process should involve multiple rounds of careful review, with a specific focus on identifying and rectifying anachronisms and inconsistencies. The meticulous attention to detail in this stage lays the foundation for a historically accurate and compelling narrative.

Fine-Tuning Historical Accuracy: Bridging the Gap Between Past and Present

While historical accuracy is a cornerstone of the genre, it's essential to strike a balance between authenticity and readability. Authors must carefully select which historical details to emphasize and how to present them to modern readers without sacrificing the integrity of the past.

A key aspect of fine-tuning historical accuracy is the integration of historical research into the narrative. Research should go beyond basic facts and encompass the nuances of the era, providing a rich and immersive backdrop for the story. Historical accuracy extends to the language used by characters, the cultural nuances, and the depiction of daily life. This level of detail not only enhances the authenticity of the novel but also enriches the reader's understanding of the historical context.

However, it's important to avoid overwhelming the narrative with an excess of historical information. While thorough research is essential, not every detail needs to be explicitly stated in the novel. Select details that are relevant to the plot, character development, or the atmosphere of the story. These chosen details should seamlessly integrate into the narrative, providing context without feeling didactic.

Dialogue is another crucial aspect of historical accuracy. Striking the balance between authentic historical language and modern accessibility is a nuanced task. While using archaic language can enhance the historical atmosphere, it should not hinder the reader's comprehension or disrupt the flow of the story. Carefully select moments to incorporate historical language, ensuring that it adds to the immersion without becoming a barrier for the reader.

Fine-tuning historical accuracy also involves understanding the perspectives and values of the historical era. Characters should behave, think, and interact based on the norms and beliefs of their time, even if those views differ from contemporary sensibilities. This authenticity allows readers to engage with the past while appreciating the historical context.

To fine-tune historical accuracy effectively, authors should seek beta readers or editors who have expertise in the historical period. These individuals can provide valuable insights, identifying areas where historical accuracy can be enhanced or where modern sensibilities inadvertently crept in. The collaboration between the author and historical experts ensures that the novel strikes the right balance between historical fidelity and modern engagement.

Seeking Feedback from Historical Experts: Refining the Authentic Narrative

The input of historical experts is a valuable resource in refining the authentic narrative of a historical novel. Their expertise can provide insights that elevate the accuracy and richness of the story, ensuring that the novel resonates with readers while honoring the past.

Historical experts can offer guidance on specific historical details, helping authors navigate the complexities of the era they are portraying. They can point out inaccuracies, suggest alternative approaches, and provide references to further enhance the research. Their input is particularly valuable in areas where the author may lack specialized knowledge, such as the intricacies of historical events, specific cultural practices, or the technical details of historical professions.

Collaborating with historical experts also helps authors capture the nuances of the historical period. These experts can shed light on the subtleties of daily life, social dynamics, and the mindset of individuals during that era. This deep understanding of the historical context allows authors to create more authentic characters and settings, immersing readers in a world that feels genuine and evocative.

When seeking feedback from historical experts, it's essential to provide them with specific questions or areas of concern. This focused approach ensures that their expertise is utilized effectively and that the author receives targeted insights. It's also important to be receptive to constructive criticism and to consider the expert's perspective when making revisions.

The involvement of historical experts is not limited to the initial drafting stage; their feedback is equally valuable during the editing and revision process. As the novel evolves, the expert's insights can help fine-tune the historical accuracy, refining the narrative to align with the expert's knowledge and the author's vision.

In conclusion, fine-tuning a historical novel requires a meticulous approach that addresses anachronisms and inconsistencies, fine-tunes historical accuracy, and seeks feedback from historical experts. By mastering these aspects of the editing and revision process, authors can create historical narratives that transport readers to the past, weaving a compelling tapestry of authenticity and imagination.

Chapter 38
Publishing and Marketing
Your Historical Novel:
A Comprehensive Guide

Publishing a historical novel is a thrilling journey that involves not only the craft of writing but also strategic decisions about the publishing route and effective marketing strategies. Finding the right publisher, choosing between traditional, hybrid, or self-publishing, navigating the historical fiction market, and building a robust author platform are essential aspects of successfully bringing your historical novel to the world. In this comprehensive guide, we'll explore each of these components in detail, equipping you with the knowledge and tools to make informed decisions and maximize the reach of your historical masterpiece.

Finding the Right Publisher for Your Work: A Crucial Decision

Choosing the right publisher is a pivotal decision that significantly impacts the trajectory of your historical novel. Publishers come in various forms, each with its own advantages and considerations. Understanding the differences between traditional, hybrid, and self-publishing can help you make an informed choice that aligns with your goals and aspirations for your historical novel.

Traditional Publishing: The Road to Literary Prestige

Traditional publishing remains a coveted path for many authors seeking literary recognition and wide distribution. Securing a publishing contract with a reputable traditional publisher can open doors to wider readership, professional editing, marketing support, and the validation of being part of the traditional literary landscape.

When seeking a traditional publisher for your historical novel, it's essential to research and target publishers who specialize in historical fiction or have a track record of publishing similar works. Tailor your submissions to each publisher, adhering to their submission guidelines, and highlighting the historical significance and market appeal of your novel.

Traditional publishing, however, comes with its challenges. It often involves a rigorous submission process, and acceptance rates can be low due to the competitive nature of the industry. Patience, perseverance, and a polished manuscript are essential when pursuing traditional publishing.

Hybrid Publishing: The Middle Ground

Hybrid publishing combines elements of both traditional and self-publishing. In a hybrid publishing model, authors often contribute to the publishing costs, and the publisher provides various services, such as editing, design, and distribution. While hybrid publishing can offer more control and a faster route to publication, it's essential to carefully review the terms and reputation of the hybrid publisher to ensure a fair arrangement.

Hybrid publishing can be a viable option for historical authors who want a degree of control over their publishing journey while still benefiting from professional services and wider distribution channels. When considering hybrid publishing, research the company's track record, reviews from other authors, and the services they offer to determine if it aligns with your needs and goals.

Self-Publishing: Empowerment and Entrepreneurship

Self-publishing has revolutionized the publishing landscape, empowering authors to bring their works directly to readers. For historical novelists, self-publishing offers creative freedom, control over every aspect of the publishing process, and the potential for higher royalties.

To self-publish your historical novel successfully, focus on producing a high-quality product. Invest in professional editing, cover design, and formatting to ensure your book meets industry standards. While self-publishing allows for more creative control, it's crucial to approach it with a professional mindset and a commitment to delivering a polished and appealing book.

Distribution is a key consideration in self-publishing. Platforms like Amazon Kindle Direct Publishing (KDP) and other self-publishing platforms offer worldwide distribution, making it easier to reach a global audience. However, authors should also explore additional distribution channels, such as other ebook retailers and print-on-demand services, to expand their reach.

Self-publishing also requires authors to take on the roles of marketer and promoter. Developing effective marketing strategies, building an author platform, and engaging with readers are essential aspects of successful self-publishing.

Navigating the Historical Fiction Market: Understanding Your Audience

Navigating the historical fiction market requires a thorough understanding of the genre, its trends, and the preferences of historical fiction enthusiasts. As a historical novelist, it's essential to position your work effectively within the market to capture the attention of your target readers.

Understanding Historical Fiction Trends: Balancing Classics and Fresh Perspectives

The historical fiction market is diverse, encompassing a wide range of subgenres, time periods, and thematic elements. Understanding current trends within the genre can help you tailor your historical novel to align with reader preferences while maintaining the uniqueness of your story.

Classic historical settings and popular time periods, such as the Tudor era, World War II, or the Victorian era, often have a dedicated readership. However, the market also welcomes fresh perspectives that explore lesser-known historical periods, cultures, and events. Balancing the allure of familiar historical settings with the intrigue of unique and unexplored aspects of history can set your novel apart.

Crafting Unique Historical Narratives: Authenticity and Creativity

While historical accuracy is paramount in historical fiction, it's essential to infuse your narrative with creativity and a unique voice. Your historical novel should transport readers to the past while offering a fresh and compelling perspective that captures their imagination.

Research is the foundation of authenticity in historical fiction. Immerse yourself in the details of the time period, including daily life, social customs, clothing, technology, and historical events. Avoid anachronisms that disrupt the historical integrity of your novel.

However, don't be afraid to take creative liberties within the bounds of historical plausibility. Characters, dialogues, and certain events can be fictionalized to serve the narrative while remaining respectful of the historical context.

Identifying Your Target Audience: Reaching Historical Enthusiasts

Knowing your target audience is essential for effective marketing and promotion. Historical fiction attracts a diverse readership, ranging from avid history buffs to readers who enjoy immersive storytelling. Identifying the key characteristics and interests of your target audience allows you to tailor your marketing efforts and connect with the readers who are most likely to resonate with your historical novel.

Consider the themes, time period, and elements of your historical novel, and think about the types of readers who would be intrigued by these aspects. Are there specific historical events or time periods that resonate with your target audience? Are there cultural or geographic elements that may appeal to certain readers? By understanding the unique appeal of your historical novel, you can create targeted marketing campaigns that speak directly to your ideal readers.

Building an Author Platform for Historical Writers: Establishing Your Presence

An author platform is a crucial asset for historical writers. It's a foundation for connecting with readers, building your brand, and promoting your historical novel effectively. A strong author platform not only helps you reach your target audience but also provides a platform for future projects and engagement with the literary community.

Author Website: Your Online Home

An author website is a central hub for your online presence. It serves as a showcase for your historical novel, a place to share information about your writing journey, and a platform for connecting with readers. When creating your author website, ensure that it reflects the historical theme of your work while being user-friendly and visually appealing.

Include sections that highlight your historical novel, your author biography, a blog or news section where you can share updates and insights, and a contact page for readers and inquiries. Consider adding resources related to the historical period of your novel, such as articles, visual references, or historical background information, to engage readers interested in the history behind your story.

Engaging with Social Media: Connect and Communicate

Social media platforms are powerful tools for building your author platform and connecting with readers. Choose platforms that align with your target audience and focus on creating engaging and informative content.

Share behind-the-scenes glimpses of your writing process, historical tidbits related to your novel, book recommendations, and interactive posts that encourage reader participation. Use hashtags related to historical fiction, writing, and the themes of your novel to expand your reach.

Engagement is key on social media. Respond to comments, participate in discussions, and build relationships with fellow authors and historical fiction enthusiasts. Authentic interaction helps you cultivate a loyal following and establishes you as a valuable member of the historical fiction community.

Connecting with Historical Enthusiasts: Events and Collaborations

Participating in events, book signings, and collaborations within the historical fiction community can significantly enhance your author platform. Look for opportunities to connect with historical enthusiasts, fellow authors, and organizations that share an interest in history.

Consider attending historical fiction conferences, book festivals, and author panels. These events allow you to meet potential readers, network with industry professionals, and gain exposure for your historical novel.

Collaborations with other historical fiction authors, historians, or bloggers can also broaden your reach. Joint promotions, guest blog posts, and shared social media activities can introduce your work to new audiences and strengthen your connections within the historical fiction community.

Leveraging Book Reviews and Endorsements: Building Credibility

Positive reviews and endorsements from reputable sources can significantly boost your credibility as a historical author. Encourage readers to leave reviews on platforms like Amazon, Goodreads, and book review blogs.

Seek professional reviews from well-known book review outlets that specialize in historical fiction. Positive reviews from respected sources can be featured on your book cover, author website, and marketing materials.

Endorsements from historical fiction experts, historians, or authors who share a similar audience can also lend credibility to your work. Reach out to these individuals and request endorsements for your historical novel. A strong endorsement can sway potential readers and increase the visibility of your book.

Effective Marketing Strategies: Promoting Your Historical Novel

Marketing your historical novel requires a strategic approach that combines online promotion, traditional marketing, and creative tactics. By leveraging a combination of digital tools, traditional promotional methods, and out-of-the-box ideas, you can maximize the visibility and impact of your historical novel.

Crafting Compelling Book Descriptions: Hooking Potential Readers

Your book description is a powerful tool for attracting readers. It's often the first introduction to your historical novel, and it needs to capture the essence of the story while enticing potential readers to dive in.

Focus on creating a book description that highlights the historical setting, introduces key characters, and teases the central conflict or mystery. Use vivid language that evokes the atmosphere of the time period and sparks curiosity.

Consider incorporating quotes or endorsements from early readers or reviews that emphasize the strengths of your historical novel. A well-crafted book description can make the difference in whether a potential reader decides to explore your work further.

Eye-Catching Cover Design: A Visual Reflection

Your book cover is a visual representation of your historical novel and plays a significant role in attracting readers. A professionally designed cover that aligns with the genre, time period, and theme of your book can significantly impact its appeal.

Invest in a high-quality book cover design that captures the historical essence of your novel. Consider historical elements, typography that complements the genre, and a design that stands out while conveying the mood or genre of the story.

When working with a cover designer, communicate the historical elements you'd like to incorporate, the emotions you want the cover to evoke, and any specific visual references from the time period. Collaborate with the designer to create a cover that aligns with your vision while meeting industry standards.

Utilizing Online Platforms: Digital Marketing

Online platforms are essential for promoting your historical novel to a global audience. Leverage the power of digital marketing to increase your book's visibility and connect with readers interested in historical fiction.

Amazon Kindle Direct Publishing (KDP): Optimize Your Presence

Amazon KDP is a central platform for self-published authors, and optimizing your presence on this platform is crucial for reaching a wide readership. Pay attention to the following elements to make the most of KDP:

- Keywords: Choose relevant keywords that reflect the historical period, themes, and subgenres of your novel. These keywords improve the discoverability of your book when readers search for historical fiction on Amazon.

- Categories: Select appropriate categories for your book, ensuring that it appears in the right subgenre and reaches readers interested in historical fiction.

- Author Central: Create an Author Central page to provide readers with information about yourself, your other works, and your historical novel. A well-crafted Author Central page enhances your credibility as an author and encourages readers to explore your catalog.

Book Promotion Websites: Effective Marketing Tools

There are various book promotion websites that specialize in promoting discounted or free books to their subscribers. Utilizing these platforms can increase the visibility of your historical novel, attract new readers, and boost sales.

Research reputable book promotion websites that cater to historical fiction or general fiction readers. Some popular book promotion sites include BookBub, Bargain Booksy, and Ereader News Today. These platforms often offer promotional packages that feature your book to their subscribers, leading to increased downloads and sales during your promotional period.

Leveraging Social Media: Engaging with Readers

Social media platforms are valuable tools for connecting with readers, promoting your historical novel, and building a loyal following. Use social media to engage with your target audience, share updates, and create a sense of community around your historical fiction.

Consider the following social media strategies:

- Regular Posts: Maintain an active presence on social media by posting regularly. Share insights about your writing process, historical tidbits, behind-the-scenes glimpses, book recommendations, and interactive content that encourages reader engagement.

- Historical Content: Tailor your social media content to the historical themes and time period of your novel. Share interesting historical facts, images, or anecdotes related to your book's setting or subject matter.

- Reader Engagement: Respond to comments, engage in discussions, and connect with fellow historical fiction enthusiasts. Building genuine connections with readers fosters a loyal following and encourages word-of-mouth promotion.

- Visual Content: Use visual content, such as graphics,

images, and videos, to enhance the visual appeal of your social media posts. Visual content is more likely to capture the attention of users scrolling through their feeds.

- Hashtags: Utilize relevant hashtags related to historical fiction, writing, book promotion, and the themes of your novel. Hashtags increase the discoverability of your posts and connect you with users interested in similar topics.

- Paid Advertising: Consider using paid advertising options on social media platforms to target specific demographics and expand your reach. Platforms like Facebook and Instagram offer targeted advertising tools that allow you to reach readers who match the profile of your ideal audience.

Engaging with Readers: Reader Interaction and Connection

Building a connection with readers is essential for long-term success as a historical novelist. Engage with your readers, listen to their feedback, and create a sense of community that encourages them to become loyal fans and advocates for your work.

Reader Interaction: Respond and Connect

When readers reach out to you, whether through email, social media, or book reviews, take the time to respond. Acknowledge their feedback, express gratitude for their support, and engage in genuine conversations. Readers appreciate authors who are accessible and responsive.

Encourage reader interaction by posing questions, hosting giveaways, or inviting readers to share their thoughts on historical topics related to your novel. Regularly interact with readers on social media, respond to comments on your blog, and participate in online discussions within the historical fiction community.

Email Newsletter: Cultivating a Loyal Fanbase

An email newsletter is a powerful tool for staying connected with your readers and cultivating a loyal fanbase. Encourage readers to sign up for your newsletter through your author website, social media, and at the end of your books.

Use your email newsletter to share updates about new releases, promotions, book events, and behind-the-scenes insights. Provide exclusive content, such as sneak peeks, bonus chapters, or historical trivia. Keep your subscribers engaged by sending regular newsletters with valuable content that keeps them excited about your historical novels.

Book Launch and Promotion: Creating Buzz

A successful book launch is a culmination of your marketing efforts, creating a buzz around your historical novel and driving initial sales. Effective book launch strategies involve pre-launch preparation, targeted promotion, and a coordinated effort to generate excitement among readers.

Pre-Launch Preparation: Build Anticipation

Prepare for your book launch well in advance by building anticipation among your audience. Consider the following pre-launch strategies:

- Cover Reveal: Create excitement by unveiling your book cover before the official launch. Share the cover on your author website, social media platforms, and in your email newsletter.

- Teasers: Share teasers, excerpts, or sneak peeks from your historical novel to pique the curiosity of potential readers. Teasers can be shared on social media, your website, and in your newsletter.

- Pre-Order Campaign: Offer a pre-order option for your historical novel. Pre-orders help generate early sales and increase visibility on retailer platforms. Incentivize pre-orders with special bonuses, such as exclusive content or discounts.

- Advance Review Copies (ARCs): Provide advance review copies of your historical novel to reviewers, bloggers, and members of your target audience. Positive reviews from early readers can create buzz and anticipation for your book.

Coordinated Promotion: Launch Activities

Launch day is a crucial moment to maximize your book's visibility and sales. Coordinate your promotional efforts to create a significant impact on launch day:

- Launch Announcement: Make a formal announcement about your book launch on your author website, social media platforms, and in your email newsletter. Include a compelling description of your historical novel, information about where readers can purchase it, and any special launch promotions or bonuses.

- Book Discounts: Consider offering a limited-time discount on the launch day to incentivize readers to purchase your historical novel. Communicate the discount through your marketing channels.

- Virtual Book Launch: Host a virtual book launch event on social media or through an online platform. Use the event to engage with readers, share insights about your historical novel, and offer prizes or giveaways.

- Coordinate with Reviewers: Encourage reviewers who received advance review copies (ARCs) to post their reviews on or around the launch day. Positive reviews on launch day can boost your book's visibility and credibility.

Post-Launch Promotion: Sustaining Momentum

After the initial launch, sustaining momentum is essential for continued sales and long-term success. Implement post-launch promotion strategies to keep your historical novel in the spotlight:

- Continued Social Media Engagement: Maintain an active presence on social media by sharing updates, engaging with readers, and promoting your historical novel in creative ways. Consider hosting contests, sharing reader testimonials, or conducting author Q&A sessions.

- Leveraging Historical Anniversaries or Events: If your historical novel aligns with specific historical anniversaries, events, or holidays, leverage these opportunities for targeted promotion. Share content related to the anniversary or event, connect it to the themes of your novel, and engage with readers who are interested in the historical context.

- Book Promotion Sites: Consider promoting your historical novel on book promotion websites, especially if you're running a limited-time promotion or discount. BookBub, Bargain Booksy, and similar platforms can help you reach a broader audience during post-launch promotion.

- Consistent Newsletter Communication: Continue sending regular email newsletters to your subscribers with updates about your writing journey, upcoming projects, and historical insights. Keep your readers engaged and excited about your future releases.

A Holistic Approach to Publishing and Marketing Your Historical Novel

Publishing and marketing a historical novel is a multifaceted endeavor that combines the craft of writing with strategic decisions and promotional efforts. Finding the right publisher, whether traditional, hybrid, or self-publishing, understanding the historical fiction market, building a robust author platform, and implementing effective marketing strategies are essential components of a successful journey.

By embracing historical accuracy, understanding reader preferences, creating a compelling author platform, and utilizing digital and traditional marketing techniques, you can maximize the impact of your historical novel, connect with a dedicated audience, and ensure that your historical masterpiece finds its place in the literary world, transporting readers to the past and leaving a lasting legacy for generations to come.

*****

The world of publishing has undergone a remarkable evolution, transforming the way authors bring their stories to readers. This article delves into the intricate choices faced by historical novelists when deciding between traditional, hybrid, and self-publishing models. With a historical novel as our focus, we'll explore the advantages, drawbacks, and considerations that authors must weigh before embarking on their publishing journey.

Traditional Publishing: Preserving Legacy

Historical novels carry readers across time, weaving tales set in bygone eras. Traditional publishing, with its legacy and established infrastructure, has been a prominent route for authors seeking to share their historical narratives.

Benefits

Traditional publishing offers authors access to experienced editors, cover designers, and marketing teams. This support ensures historical accuracy, proper language usage, and appealing visual representation. Established publishing houses hold sway in the industry, facilitating shelf presence in brick-and-mortar bookstores and libraries. This visibility can attract history enthusiasts and readers looking for well-vetted historical narratives.

Drawbacks

However, the traditional path is not without its challenges. Historical novels often demand meticulous research, which can be slowed down by traditional publishing's lengthy submission and revision processes. Additionally, authors might find their creative control limited, as publishers make design and marketing decisions that may not perfectly align with the novel's historical nuances.

Control

Authors relinquish substantial control to publishers in this model, particularly in design and marketing. The historical authenticity of the novel might be subject to interpretation by professionals with differing visions.

Distribution and Marketing

Traditional publishers boast extensive distribution networks, ensuring that historical novels reach bookstores and libraries globally. Marketing campaigns, including book tours and advertisements, can enhance the novel's visibility.

Financial Implications

Authors are often paid advances against royalties, which can provide financial stability. However, royalties themselves might not be as substantial due to the involvement of various intermediaries.

Hybrid Publishing: Bridging Histories

Hybrid publishing combines elements of traditional and self-publishing, offering historical novelists a middle ground that retains both professional expertise and creative control.

Benefits

For historical novelists seeking more input in design and marketing, hybrid publishing provides a compromise. Authors receive services such as professional editing and cover design while retaining a say in decisions that impact historical accuracy.

Drawbacks

However, the hybrid route is not without its challenges. Costs can be higher than traditional publishing, as authors often invest upfront in various services. The quality of services can vary among hybrid publishers, necessitating thorough research.

Control

Authors have a higher degree of control compared to traditional publishing. They can influence decisions about cover design, formatting, and marketing strategies, ensuring historical integrity.

Distribution and Marketing

Hybrid publishers employ a blend of traditional and digital distribution channels. Marketing strategies vary widely, requiring authors to take a more active role in promotion.

Financial Implications

Authors share some of the financial responsibility upfront but retain a larger portion of royalties compared to traditional publishing. Financial returns are tied to the book's success.

Self-Publishing: Scripting Your Narrative

Self-publishing empowers historical novelists to take full control of their narrative, ensuring that their creative vision and historical accuracy remain uncompromised.

Benefits

The allure of self-publishing lies in its unprecedented creative freedom. Historical novelists can swiftly publish their works, reaching a global audience through digital platforms. Royalty rates in self-publishing are often higher than traditional models, allowing authors to reap more from each sale.

Drawbacks

However, self-publishing has its challenges. Without professional editing and design, historical novels can suffer from issues of quality. Authors must also take on the entirety of marketing and distribution, which can be daunting without industry connections.

Control

Self-published authors hold complete control over their work, from content to cover design. This extends to pricing, release dates, and marketing strategies, ensuring historical accuracy remains unaltered.

Distribution and Marketing

Self-publishing relies heavily on digital platforms like Amazon Kindle Direct Publishing (KDP) for distribution. Success hinges on an author's ability to build an online presence and engage in effective self-promotion.

Financial Implications

While self-published authors have the potential for higher earnings per sale, the initial investments in editing, cover design, and marketing can impact overall profitability.

Comparing the Models for Historical Novels

When navigating the choice between traditional, hybrid, and self-publishing for historical novels, several key considerations emerge.

Control and Historical Authenticity

The historical accuracy of a novel might be better preserved through self-publishing, where authors retain control over every aspect of their work. Hybrid publishing allows for a balance between creative control and professional support, while traditional publishing leans more toward professional expertise.

Distribution and Reach

Traditional publishing offers the broadest distribution network, but self-publishing's digital reach is global. Hybrid publishing falls in between, with distribution methods varying by publisher.

Financial Implications

Authors seeking upfront financial support may prefer traditional or hybrid publishing due to advances, while self-publishing offers higher long-term royalties. However, financial success in self-publishing requires proactive marketing efforts.

Quality and Professionalism

Traditional publishing and reputable hybrid publishers ensure high-quality editing and design, critical for historical novels. Self-published authors must invest in these services to meet the same standards.

Time-to-Market

Self-publishing offers the quickest route to market, making it suitable for authors eager to share their historical narratives promptly.

Selecting the right publishing model for a historical novel requires a careful evaluation of an author's goals, resources, and priorities. Traditional publishing preserves legacy, hybrid publishing offers a compromise, and self-publishing empowers authors to shape their narrative. As historical novelists embark on their publishing journey, they must consider their creative vision, financial aspirations, and dedication to historical authenticity. Through an informed choice, they can navigate the ever-changing seas of the publishing world and share their historical stories with readers around the globe.

*****

Is a Hybrid Press and a
Vanity Press the Same Thing?

Vanity presses and hybrid presses are two distinct models in the publishing industry, each offering authors different approaches to getting their work into print. It's important to understand the differences between them before making a decision on which route to take.

Vanity Press

A vanity press, also known as a subsidy press or author services company, is a type of publishing company that offers services to authors in exchange for payment. In the traditional vanity press model, authors pay a fee upfront to have their book published. These fees often cover services such as editing, formatting, cover design, printing, and distribution. In return, the vanity press publishes the book and provides copies to the author. The primary characteristic of a vanity press is that the author bears the financial responsibility for the production and publication of the book.

Key Features of Vanity Press:

1. **Author Pays:** Authors pay a fee to have their book published.
2. **Financial Responsibility:** The author covers the costs of editing, design, printing, and other production aspects.
3. **Minimal Selection Process:** Vanity presses often accept most manuscripts without rigorous editorial evaluation.
4. **Limited Distribution:** Distribution might be limited to the author purchasing copies directly or through the publisher's platform.
5. **Profit Model:** The publisher's main revenue comes from the fees paid by authors, rather than book sales.

Vanity presses have garnered criticism over the years due to concerns about the quality of their services, the lack of editorial standards, and the potential for authors to invest significant money without necessarily achieving widespread success or recognition.

Hybrid Press

A hybrid press, on the other hand, combines elements of traditional publishing and self-publishing. It aims to provide a middle ground between the two models, offering authors a more selective and curated approach while still involving them in the publishing process.

Key Features of Hybrid Press:

1. **Selective Process:** Hybrid presses usually have a submission and selection process. They evaluate manuscripts for quality and market potential.
2. **Shared Costs:** Authors may contribute financially to cover some production costs, but the publisher also invests in the book's publication.
3. **Professional Services:** Hybrid presses typically provide professional services like editing, design, and distribution.
4. **Royalties:** Authors often receive royalties from book sales, with a more equitable distribution compared to vanity presses.
5. **Control and Collaboration:** Authors have more input into the design, marketing, and distribution aspects while benefiting from the publisher's expertise.

The main distinction between hybrid presses and vanity presses lies in their commitment to quality, editorial standards, and a more balanced approach to cost-sharing and revenue distribution. Hybrid presses aim to offer authors a legitimate publishing avenue that blends elements of traditional publishing support with a collaborative and more author-friendly model.

While both vanity presses and hybrid presses involve authors contributing financially to the publication of their books, hybrid presses tend to prioritize quality, selection, and collaboration more than vanity presses. Authors considering these options should carefully research and evaluate the reputation and services of any publishing company they are considering, regardless of whether it falls under the vanity or hybrid press category.

For a look at an award-winning hybrid press exclusively for Historical Fiction, visit www.historiumpress.com or www.thehistoricalfictioncompany.com/historium-press

Chapter 39
The Future of Historical Fiction

Historical fiction has long held a special place in the literary world, transporting readers to bygone eras and illuminating forgotten tales. In this ever-evolving landscape, where technology and storytelling intersect, the future of historical fiction is a subject of fascination and speculation. This article explores the trends, innovations, and timeless qualities that are shaping the genre's trajectory.

Historical fiction is no stranger to technology's embrace. With the advent of digital tools, authors are now able to meticulously research and recreate historical settings with unprecedented accuracy. Immersive technologies such as virtual reality (VR) and augmented reality (AR) allow readers to step into the shoes of historical characters and explore historical landscapes like never before. This integration of technology deepens the reader's engagement and enhances their understanding of the past.

The future of historical fiction is becoming increasingly diverse, shedding light on untold stories and marginalized voices from history. Authors are exploring narratives from different cultural backgrounds, genders, and socio-economic classes, enriching the genre with a tapestry of perspectives. This inclusivity not only broadens readers' horizons but also provides a more comprehensive understanding of historical events.

Boundaries between genres are becoming porous, and historical fiction is no exception. Authors are blending historical elements with speculative fiction, fantasy, and science fiction, creating alternate historical realities that challenge conventional narratives. This fusion of genres adds an element of surprise and unpredictability to historical storytelling, appealing to readers seeking fresh and innovative narratives.

The future of historical fiction involves breathing new life into well-known historical figures. Authors are exploring the inner lives and motivations of historical personalities, painting multidimensional portraits that challenge simplistic characterizations. This nuanced approach humanizes historical figures and invites readers to engage with their struggles, desires, and complexities.

In an era where information is readily accessible, historical fiction is tasked with discovering and resurrecting lesser-known events and characters. Authors are mining archives, diaries, and oral histories to unveil hidden stories that offer fresh perspectives on familiar eras. This commitment to unearthing forgotten narratives injects a sense of discovery into the genre, satisfying readers' hunger for untold tales.

The future of historical fiction lies in grappling with the ethical and moral dilemmas of the past. Authors are delving into complex historical events, examining the choices and consequences faced by individuals during critical moments in history. This exploration of moral ambiguity adds depth to characters and invites readers to reflect on the choices they would make in similar situations.

While historical fiction transports readers to the past, its relevance to the present is unmistakable. Authors are drawing parallels between historical events and contemporary issues, inviting readers to contemplate the cyclical nature of history and the lessons it holds for our times. This resonance bridges the gap between past and present, fostering a deeper connection with the narrative.

The core of historical fiction lies in its portrayal of universal human emotions that transcend time and place. Love, loss, ambition, and fear are emotions that have been experienced by individuals throughout history. By tapping into these timeless feelings, historical fiction resonates with readers on a profound level, reminding them of the shared human experience.

The future of historical fiction embraces the challenge of authentically capturing the essence of eras long gone. Authors meticulously research not only historical facts but also the cultural nuances, language, and societal norms of the past. This attention to detail immerses readers in the sights, sounds, and textures of historical periods, creating a sensory-rich experience that transports them through time.

As we gaze into the future of historical fiction, we see a genre that is both honoring its roots and venturing boldly into uncharted territories. Trends in technology, inclusivity, and genre-blending are reshaping how historical stories are told. Authors are pushing the boundaries of the genre, unearthing forgotten stories, and delving into ethical complexities. Yet, amidst all these innovations, historical fiction remains timeless, resonating with readers through universal emotions and the essence of eras long past. As readers continue to seek refuge in the pages of historical fiction, they are reminded that the past not only shapes our present but also holds a mirror to our shared humanity.

Chapter 40
Learning from Other Classic Writers

*****

Cormac McCarthy

Incorporating the phenomenal writing style of Cormac McCarthy into your historical novel requires a deep understanding of his unique narrative techniques and the essence of historical storytelling. McCarthy's prose is marked by its sparse yet evocative language, vivid imagery, and exploration of profound themes. Here's how you can infuse your historical novel with elements reminiscent of Cormac McCarthy's writing style:

McCarthy is renowned for his realistic and impactful dialogue. His characters' conversations often convey deeper meanings and subtext. Incorporate this into your historical novel by crafting dialogues that are both authentic to the era and emotionally charged. Focus on what remains unsaid, allowing the gaps in dialogue to reveal character motivations and the tensions of the time.

McCarthy's writing is characterized by its economy of words and poetic phrasing. Use descriptive language that paints vivid imagery without unnecessary embellishments. Create scenes that rely on the power of suggestion, enabling readers to engage their imagination and immerse themselves in the historical setting.

In McCarthy's novels, landscapes often take on a life of their own, reflecting the characters' journeys and internal struggles. In your historical novel, treat the historical setting as a character with its own personality. Describe the land, weather, and natural elements in a way that resonates with the emotional atmosphere of the story.

McCarthy's characters frequently navigate isolation and solitude in their journeys. In your historical novel, delve into the emotional isolation that historical figures might have experienced due to their circumstances. Explore how the era's societal norms and geographical constraints impact your characters' relationships and personal growth.

Cormac McCarthy's characters often have complex and troubled pasts. Develop historical characters with multifaceted backgrounds, secrets, and inner conflicts that shape their decisions and interactions. Reveal these layers gradually, allowing readers to uncover the depth of your characters' motivations.

McCarthy's novels frequently delve into moral ambiguity and ethical dilemmas. Infuse your historical novel with similar depth by placing your characters in situations that challenge their values and force them to confront difficult choices. This exploration adds complexity and authenticity to the historical narrative.

Symbolism is a hallmark of McCarthy's writing. Incorporate symbolic elements that resonate with the themes of your historical novel. These symbols can be objects, animals, or recurring motifs that enrich the story's meaning and offer readers a deeper layer of interpretation.

McCarthy's novels often confront violence and brutality, mirroring the harsh realities of life. While historical novels may not require the same level of graphic violence, you can engage with the darker aspects of the era. Address social injustices, conflicts, and the struggles faced by individuals in the historical context.

McCarthy provides minimalist character descriptions, allowing readers to visualize characters based on their actions and dialogue. Follow this approach in your historical novel by revealing characters' traits and appearances through their behavior and interactions rather than lengthy exposition.

McCarthy's themes often transcend time, making his narratives feel timeless. Incorporate themes in your historical novel that resonate with contemporary issues, connecting the past to the present and inviting readers to reflect on the continuity of human experiences.

Remember that while infusing elements of Cormac McCarthy's style, your voice as an author should shine through. By drawing inspiration from his techniques and themes, you can create a historical novel that captures the essence of both the past and the literary greatness that McCarthy exemplifies.

*****

Herman Melville

Herman Melville, the renowned author of "Moby-Dick," possesses insights that can greatly benefit writers of historical fiction. His skill in crafting captivating first lines and his approach to historical storytelling offer valuable lessons. Here's what Herman Melville can teach writers about writing historical fiction and using captivating first lines:

Melville's historical novels, like "Benito Cereno" and "White-Jacket," demonstrate the importance of thorough research. Immerse yourself in the era you're portraying to accurately capture the nuances of the time, including language, customs, social structures, and political landscapes.

His historical fiction balances imagination with historical accuracy. While he creates fictional characters and events, they are firmly grounded in the historical context. Strike a similar balance, blending creative storytelling with authenticity to bring the past to life.

Melville's works often delve into moral and philosophical complexities. Use historical fiction as a lens to explore ethical dilemmas and societal issues relevant to the era. This adds depth to your narrative and invites readers to reflect on the parallels between past and present.

And his characters possess authentic voices that reflect their backgrounds and perspectives. Through dialogue and narration, capture the linguistic nuances and idioms of the historical period, enhancing the credibility of your characters and setting.

Melville's exploration of universal themes—such as human nature, power, and obsession—transcends time. Infuse your historical fiction with themes that resonate across eras, allowing readers to connect with the emotional and philosophical aspects of the story.

Without a doubt, his first lines often pique readers' curiosity. Begin your historical fiction with a statement, question, or image that intrigues readers and encourages them to delve further into the narrative. Create a sense of mystery or anticipation that compels them to continue reading.

His first lines often set the mood and atmosphere of the story. Use descriptive language to create a vivid sense of the historical setting, transporting readers to the era you're portraying. This sensory immersion draws readers into the world of your novel.

They also hint at the conflicts or challenges that characters will face. Introduce a glimpse of the central conflict, tension, or dilemma to create anticipation and suspense. This approach hooks readers by promising them an engaging and intriguing narrative.

His first lines often introduce strong, enigmatic, or intriguing characters. Begin your historical fiction by introducing a character with a distinctive personality, motivation, or situation. This can spark readers' interest and make them eager to learn more about the character's journey.

Succinct yet impactful. Craft your opening line with economy of language, choosing words that convey a strong impression while leaving room for readers' imagination. A well-crafted concise line can have a lasting impact and hint at the thematic elements of the story. Align your opening line with the overarching themes of your historical novel. This creates a sense of cohesion and resonance that enhances readers' engagement.

Incorporating Herman Melville's approach to historical fiction and his mastery of captivating first lines can elevate your own writing. By combining meticulous research, imaginative storytelling, exploration of universal themes, and the art of crafting compelling openings, you'll be better equipped to craft immersive historical narratives that capture readers' attention from the very first word.

*****

The journey of becoming a skilled writer is a dynamic process that involves a multifaceted set of skills and experiences. While many factors contribute to the development of writing prowess, one cornerstone stands unwaveringly: the act of reading. To truly excel as a writer, one must embrace the role of an avid and discerning reader. This article delves into the profound connection between reading and writing, highlighting why aspiring writers must cultivate their reading habits to flourish in their craft.

Writing is more than just the arrangement of words on a page; it is a form of artistry that necessitates an understanding of language, rhythm, structure, and nuance. These foundational elements are cultivated not only through the practice of writing itself but also through the immersive experience of reading. By exposing oneself to diverse styles, genres, and voices, aspiring writers gain insights into the intricate mechanics of language and storytelling.

Reading opens the door to unexplored worlds and perspectives, inspiring creativity in writers. Exposure to a wide range of literature nurtures creativity by introducing new concepts, ideas, and possibilities. Whether it's through a fantasy realm, a historical period, or a character's internal monologue, reading provides a rich tapestry of inspiration that can be woven into one's own writing.

Effective writing relies on a rich and varied vocabulary to convey thoughts and emotions with precision. Reading exposes writers to an array of words, phrases, and expressions that expand their linguistic repertoire. A well-crafted sentence can capture a reader's imagination, and the ability to employ a diverse vocabulary empowers writers to do just that.

From the artful deployment of literary devices to the construction of compelling plotlines, reading acquaints writers with the subtleties of narrative technique. Analyzing how other authors craft suspense, evoke emotions, and create tension offers valuable lessons that can be applied to one's own storytelling endeavors.

Effective writing is not just about inspiration; it requires a critical eye for detail. Reading encourages analytical thinking as readers evaluate character development, plot twists, pacing, and thematic resonance. This practice of critical analysis naturally extends to one's own work, allowing writers to identify areas for improvement and refinement.

Every writer aspires to discover their unique voice—a distinctive style that resonates with readers. Reading a diverse array of authors aids in this discovery by exposing writers to a myriad of voices, allowing them to identify elements that resonate with their own sensibilities. The synthesis of these influences contributes to the formation of a writer's voice.

Every writer encounters periods of creative drought. Reading acts as a wellspring of rejuvenation during these moments. Engaging with literature provides a mental reset, rejuvenating one's creativity and providing fresh perspectives that can inspire new ideas and approaches.

The assertion that to be a good writer, one must be a good reader is not a trite adage but a profound truth. Reading nurtures the foundations of writing craft, stimulates creativity, cultivates vocabulary, and enhances critical analysis. The interplay between reading and writing is a symbiotic relationship, where each endeavor enriches and enhances the other. Aspiring writers should embrace the role of an active reader, recognizing that every page turned is a step towards honing their own literary prowess. Through the timeless act of reading, writers embark on a continuous journey of growth, discovery, and mastery.

What have you read?

What book impacted you the most?

How can I use this book to find my own voice?

Top 100 Best Historical Books of All Time:

Creating a definitive list of the top 100 best historical books of all time is a subjective endeavor, as different readers have varying preferences and criteria for what constitutes a "best" book. However, I can certainly provide you with a selection of influential and highly regarded historical books from a variety of eras and genres. Keep in mind that this list is not exhaustive and is presented in no particular order:

1. "War and Peace" by Leo Tolstoy
2. "The Odyssey" by Homer
3. "A Tale of Two Cities" by Charles Dickens
4. "One Hundred Years of Solitude" by Gabriel García Márquez
5. "To Kill a Mockingbird" by Harper Lee
6. "Pride and Prejudice" by Jane Austen
7. "1984" by George Orwell
8. "The Book Thief" by Markus Zusak
9. "The Grapes of Wrath" by John Steinbeck
10. "The Name of the Rose" by Umberto Eco
11. "All the Light We Cannot See" by Anthony Doerr
12. "The Nightingale" by Kristin Hannah
13. "Gone with the Wind" by Margaret Mitchell
14. "The Pillars of the Earth" by Ken Follett
15. "The Things They Carried" by Tim O'Brien
16. "The Help" by Kathryn Stockett
17. "The Kite Runner" by Khaled Hosseini

18. "The Count of Monte Cristo" by Alexandre Dumas
19. "The Great Gatsby" by F. Scott Fitzgerald
20. "The Scarlet Letter" by Nathaniel Hawthorne
21. "Brave New World" by Aldous Huxley
22. "The Diary of a Young Girl" by Anne Frank
23. "Maus" by Art Spiegelman
24. "The Three Musketeers" by Alexandre Dumas
25. "The Song of Achilles" by Madeline Miller
26. "The Historian" by Elizabeth Kostova
27. "Wolf Hall" by Hilary Mantel
28. "The Red Tent" by Anita Diamant
29. "The Secret History" by Donna Tartt
30. "The Picture of Dorian Gray" by Oscar Wilde
31. "The Remains of the Day" by Kazuo Ishiguro
32. "The Amazing Adventures of Kavalier & Clay" by Michael Chabon
33. "Cold Mountain" by Charles Frazier
34. "Memoirs of a Geisha" by Arthur Golden
35. "The Miniaturist" by Jessie Burton
36. "The Shadow of the Wind" by Carlos Ruiz Zafón
37. "Les Misérables" by Victor Hugo
38. "The Catcher in the Rye" by J.D. Salinger
39. "The White Queen" by Philippa Gregory
40. "The Martian" by Andy Weir
41. "The Road" by Cormac McCarthy
42. "The Alchemist" by Paulo Coelho
43. "Empire Falls" by Richard Russo
44. "The Master and Margarita" by Mikhail Bulgakov
45. "The Devil in the White City" by Erik Larson
46. "The Luminaries" by Eleanor Catton
47. "The Power of One" by Bryce Courtenay
48. "The Joy Luck Club" by Amy Tan
49. "Siddhartha" by Hermann Hesse
50. "A Farewell to Arms" by Ernest Hemingway

51. "The Wind-Up Bird Chronicle" by Haruki Murakami
52. "Roots" by Alex Haley
53. "Doctor Zhivago" by Boris Pasternak
54. "The Goldfinch" by Donna Tartt
55. "The Name of the Wind" by Patrick Rothfuss
56. "The Master and Commander" by Patrick O'Brian
57. "The Hunchback of Notre-Dame" by Victor Hugo
58. "The Bell Jar" by Sylvia Plath
59. "The Poisonwood Bible" by Barbara Kingsolver
60. "The Handmaid's Tale" by Margaret Atwood
61. "Outlander" by Diana Gabaldon
62. "The Secret Garden" by Frances Hodgson Burnett
63. "Half of a Yellow Sun" by Chimamanda Ngozi Adichie
64. "The Boy in the Striped Pajamas" by John Boyne
65. "The Color Purple" by Alice Walker
66. "The Picture of Dorian Gray" by Oscar Wilde
67. "The Shining" by Stephen King
68. "A Clockwork Orange" by Anthony Burgess
69. "The Metamorphosis" by Franz Kafka
70. "The Jungle" by Upton Sinclair
71. "The Da Vinci Code" by Dan Brown
72. "The Stand" by Stephen King
73. "The Brief Wondrous Life of Oscar Wao" by Junot Díaz
74. "The Silence of the Girls" by Pat Barker
75. "The Song of Roland" by Unknown
76. "The Stranger" by Albert Camus
77. "The Once and Future King" by T.H. White
78. "A Place Called Freedom" by Ken Follett
79. "The Clan of the Cave Bear" by Jean M. Auel
80. "The Road to Wigan Pier" by George Orwell
81. "The City of Ember" by Jeanne DuPrau
82. "The Maze Runner" by James Dashner

83."The Silver Pigs" by Lindsey Davis
84."The Historian" by Elizabeth Kostova
85."In the Woods" by Tana French
86."The Historian" by Elizabeth Kostova
87."The Last Kingdom" by Bernard Cornwell
88."The Da Vinci Code" by Dan Brown
89."The Name of the Rose" by Umberto Eco
90."The Alienist" by Caleb Carr
91."The Alice Network" by Kate Quinn
92."The Other Boleyn Girl" by Philippa Gregory
93."The Nightingale" by Kristin Hannah
94."The Bronze Horseman" by Paullina Simons
95."The Given Day" by Dennis Lehane
96."The Lilac Girls" by Martha Hall Kelly
97."The Winds of War" by Herman Wouk
98."The Source" by James A. Michener
99."The Fountains of Silence" by Ruta Sepetys
100."The Tattooist of Auschwitz" by Heather Morris

Remember that this list is by no means exhaustive, and there are countless other historical books that have left an indelible mark on literature. Your personal preferences, interests, and cultural background may influence your own list of favorites.

Chapter 41

In My Words

In the tumultuous expanse of human existence, there lies a realm where past and present intertwine, where the echoes of history resonate in the hearts and minds of those who dare to tread upon it. This realm, my dear reader, is none other than the sphere of historical fiction—a genre I adore and that possesses a unique potency to shape our lives as writers, surmount the challenges of our modern world, and bestow upon us the profound gratification of artistic creation.

Historical fiction, like a masterful tapestry, weaves together threads of the past and the present, offering readers a glimpse into worlds that once were. As writers, the impact of this genre upon our lives is undeniable. We, the scribes of ink and imagination, are tasked with breathing life into bygone eras, revitalizing characters whose souls have long been dormant. Through meticulous research and the alchemy of prose, we resurrect the past, capturing its essence for the modern eye.

The influence of historical fiction extends beyond the mere act of writing; it resonates within our very beings. To pen a historical narrative is to embark upon a journey of discovery —a voyage into the recesses of history, a quest for authenticity, and an exploration of the universal truths that transcend time. As writers, we evolve into archaeologists of the human experience, unearthing forgotten tales, perspectives, and lessons that illuminate our own existence.

Ah, the challenges that assail the modern writer—like tempestuous winds that threaten to extinguish the creative flame. In this age of constant connectivity and ephemeral attention spans, we grapple with distractions that pull us away from the sanctuary of our thoughts. The rapid pace of life demands instant gratification, often leaving little room for the slow gestation of our narratives.

Yet, it is precisely in this maelstrom that historical fiction emerges as a refuge—a steadfast anchor that grounds us amidst the chaos. As we immerse ourselves in the depths of the past, the immediacy of the present fades, and we find solace in the embrace of history. We embrace patience, for we know that the creation of historical fiction demands time— time to research, to reflect, and to craft narratives that possess the resonance of the ages.

In the ceaseless pursuit of artistic fulfillment, historical fiction offers a profound and timeless satisfaction. As writers, we derive immense joy from the act of shaping a world that once was, fashioning characters whose struggles mirror our own, and imparting wisdom that transcends eras. The pleasure is twofold: the delight of creation and the realization that our narratives contribute to the preservation of the human story.

Through the challenges and triumphs, we come to understand that the intrinsic value of writing lies not merely in its end result, but in the very process of creation. The satisfaction of crafting worlds and breathing life into characters forms an intimate bond between writer and narrative. The final manuscript, like a monument erected to honor the past, stands as a testament to our dedication, resilience, and passion for storytelling.

As I conclude this contemplation, I am reminded of the ceaseless journey that is the writer's existence. We are travelers, navigators of the human experience, tasked with the noble duty of capturing fragments of existence and immortalizing them in ink. Historical fiction, with its allure and challenges, beckons us to delve into the annals of time, to engage in a dance with history itself.

And so, my fellow writers, let us embrace the transformative power of historical fiction—a genre that connects us to our roots, emboldens us to face the modern world's trials, and fills our souls with the ineffable satisfaction of artistic creation. Let us continue to pen stories that transcend time, stories that remind us of our shared humanity, and stories that illuminate the intricate tapestry of existence that binds us all.

ABOUT THE AUTHOR

D K Marley (Dee Marley) is an award-winning historical author of six historical novels, a 35+ year experienced graphic designer and owner of White Rabbit Arts, and marketer, as well as the CEO and editor-in-chief of the Historical Fiction Companies: The Historical Fiction Company, Historium Press, Historical Times Magazine, History Bards Podcast, The HFC Youtube Channel, and The Hist Fic Chickie Blog.

She uses her experience as a historical author to help other aspiring authors, as well as seasoned authors excel exclusively in this much-loved genre. She is a member of the Historial Novel Society, and has her own Facebook, Instagram, and Twitter groups with well over 8000 followers at the date of publication of this book.

To learn more about Dee's novels, you can visit her FB page at:

www.facebook.com/therealdkmarley.author

Twitter: @histficcompany and @histtimesmag

Instagram: @histficcompany and @histtimesmag

Facebook: www.facebook.com/thehistoricalfictioncompany

www.facebook.com/historicaltimesmagazine

www.facebook.com/historiumpress

D. K. Marley

www.facebook.com/groups/historicalfictionbookclub

Official websites:

www.thehistoricalfictioncompany.com

www.historicaltimes.org

www.historiumpress.com

www.historiumpress.com

www.ingramcontent.com/pod-product-compliance
Lightning Source LLC
Chambersburg PA
CBHW060914120626
46553CB00001B/319